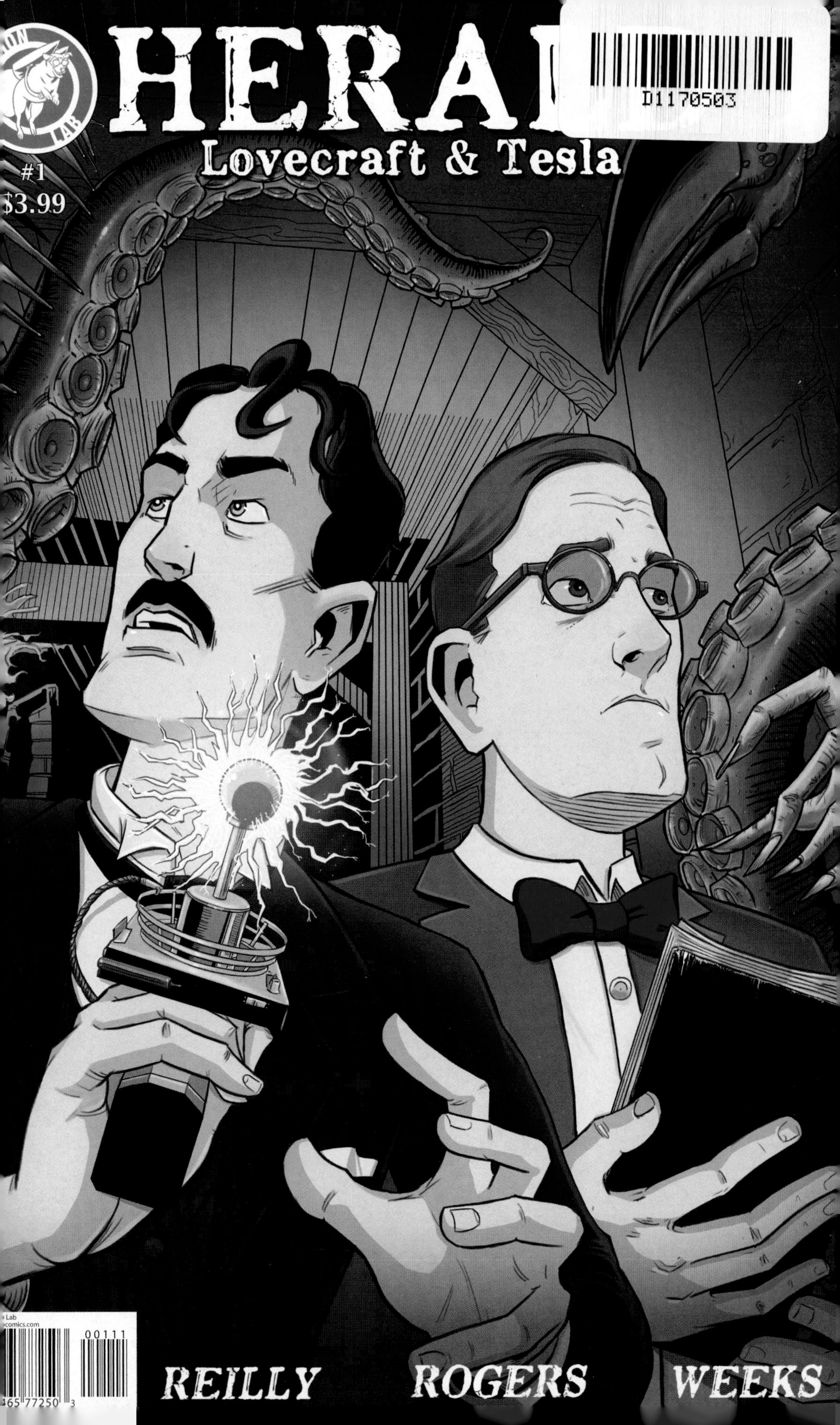
HERA
Lovecraft & Tesla
#1
$3.99
REILLY
ROGERS
WEEKS

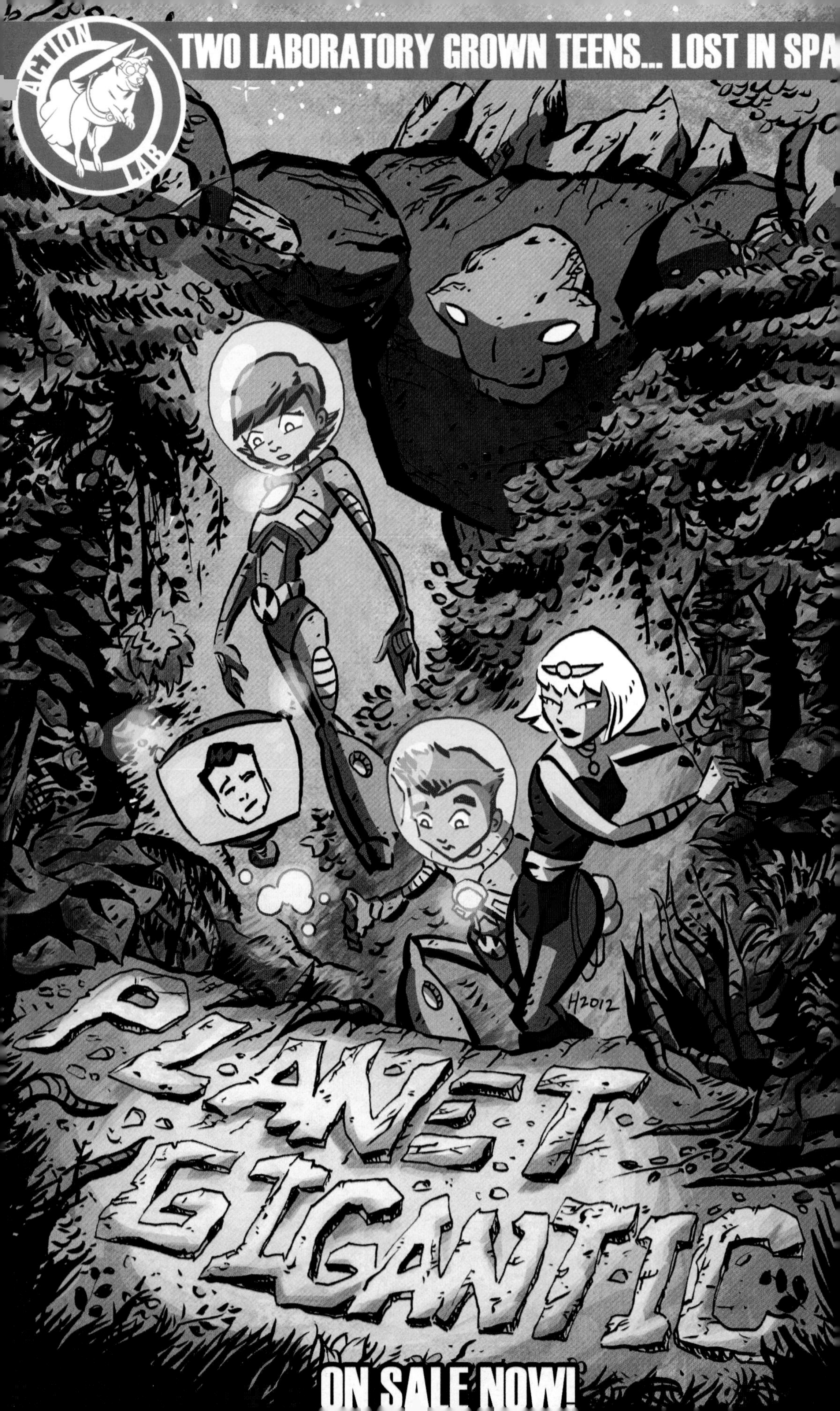
ACTION LAB
TWO LABORATORY GROWN TEENS... LOST IN SPA
H2012
PLANET GIGANTIC
ON SALE NOW!

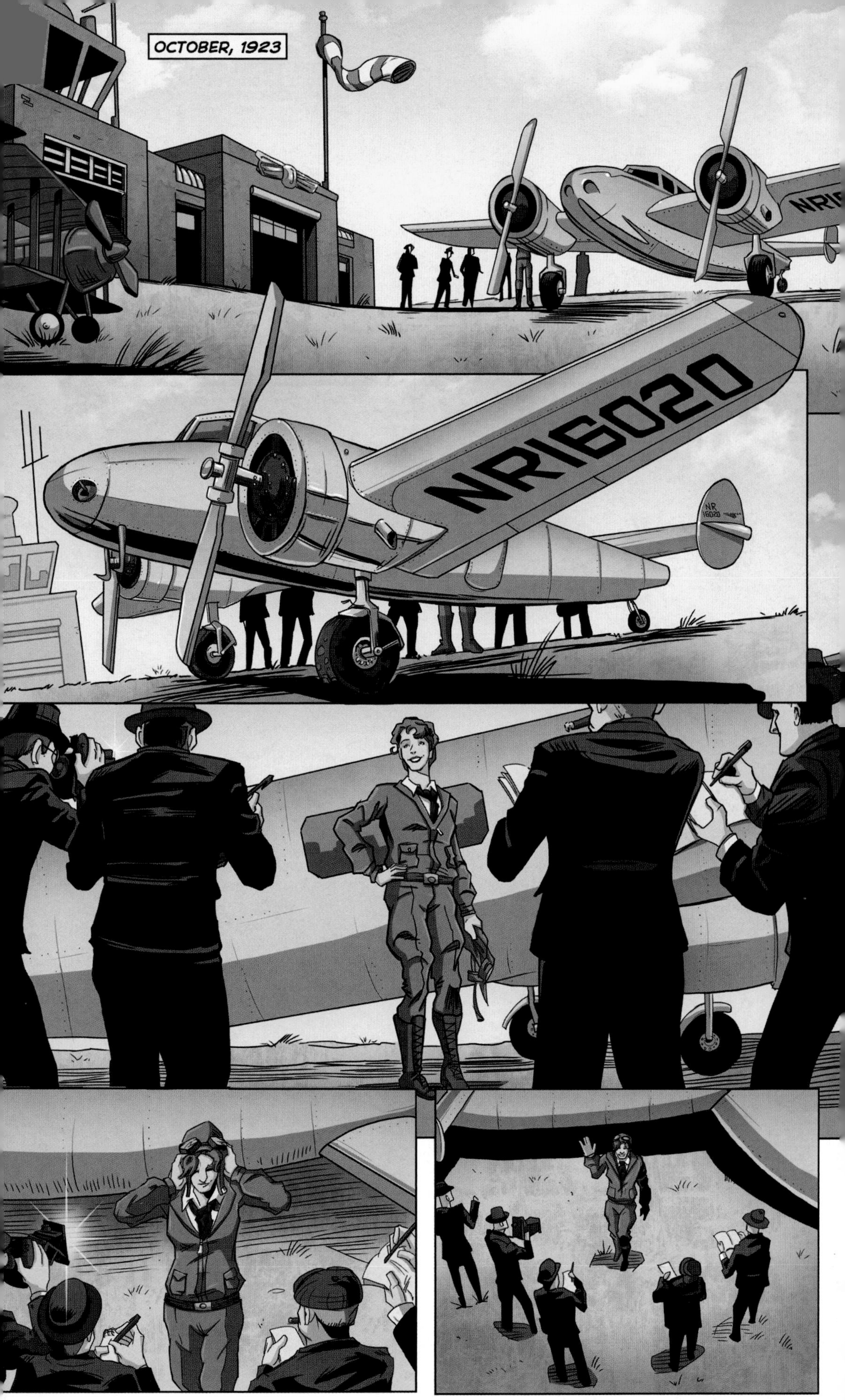
OCTOBER, 1923
NR16020

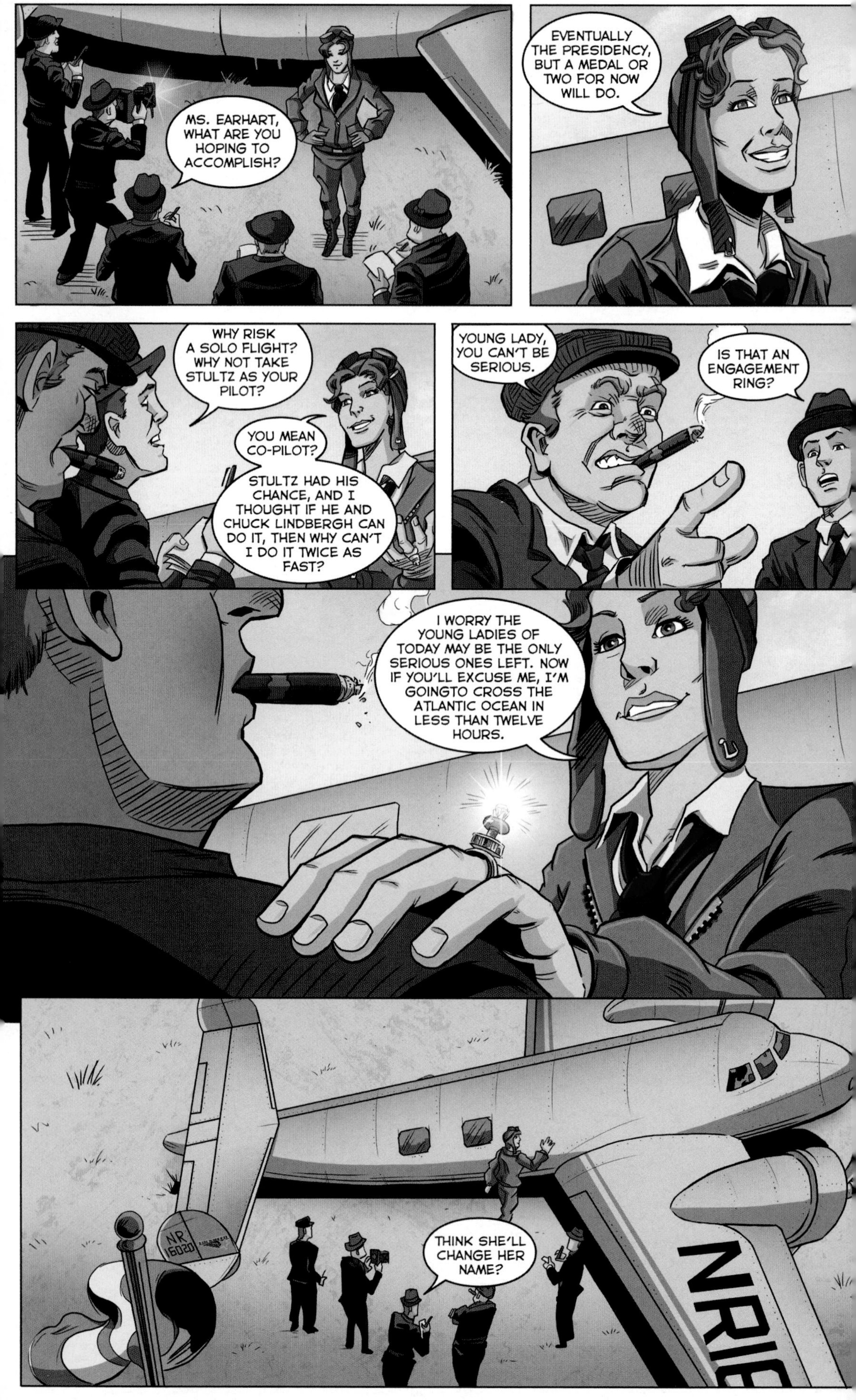
MS. EARHART, WHAT ARE YOU HOPING TO ACCOMPLISH?
EVENTUALLY THE PRESIDENCY, BUT A MEDAL OR TWO FOR NOW WILL DO.
WHY RISK A SOLO FLIGHT? WHY NOT TAKE STULTZ AS YOUR PILOT?
YOU MEAN CO-PILOT?
STULTZ HAD HIS CHANCE, AND I THOUGHT IF HE AND CHUCK LINDBERGH CAN DO IT, THEN WHY CAN'T I DO IT TWICE AS FAST?
YOUNG LADY, YOU CAN'T BE SERIOUS.
IS THAT AN ENGAGEMENT RING?
I WORRY THE YOUNG LADIES OF TODAY MAY BE THE ONLY SERIOUS ONES LEFT. NOW IF YOU'LL EXCUSE ME, I'M GOINGTO CROSS THE ATLANTIC OCEAN IN LESS THAN TWELVE HOURS.
NR 16020
THINK SHE'LL CHANGE HER NAME?
NR16

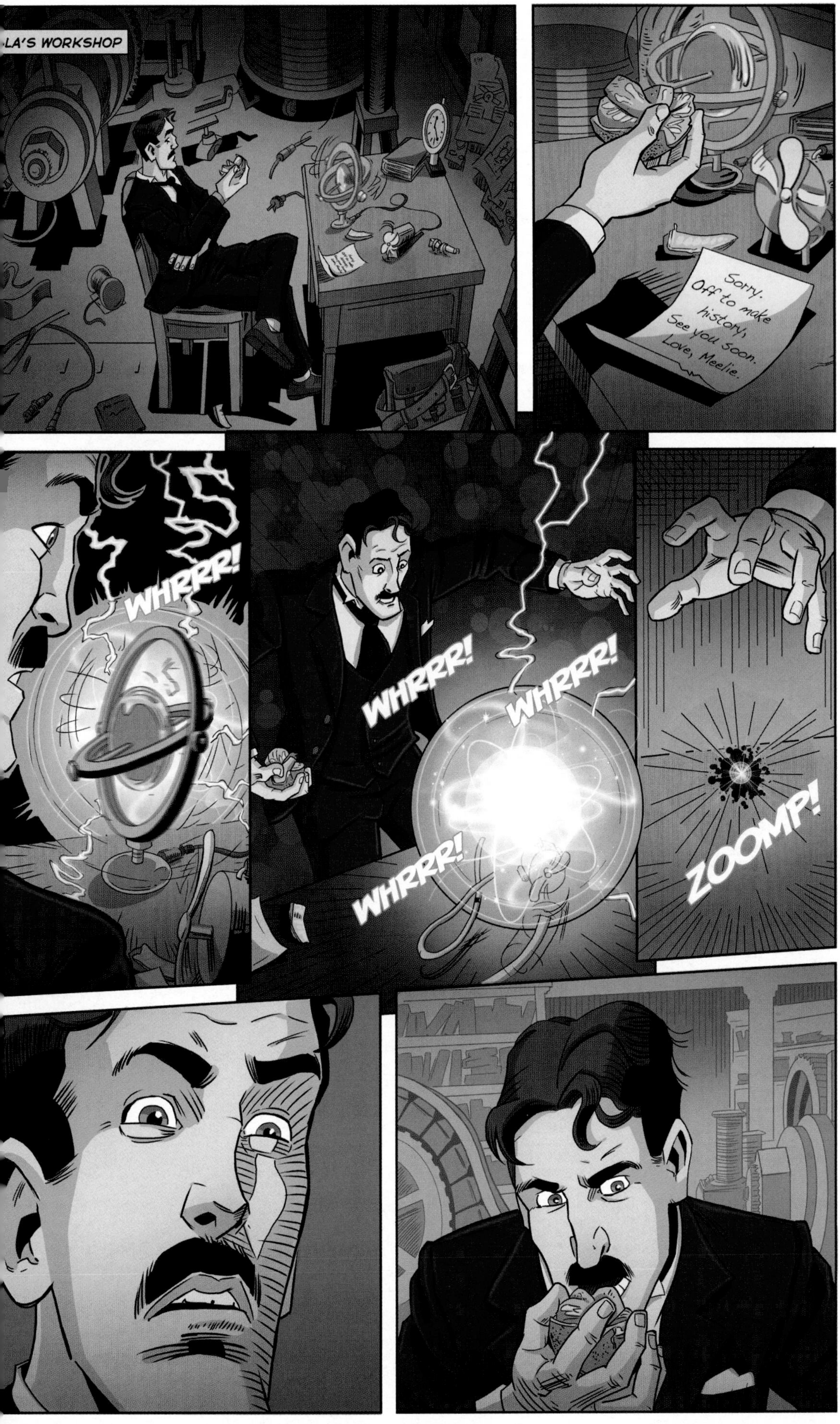

LA'S WORKSHOP
Sorry. Off to make history. See you soon. Love, Meelie.
WHRRR!
WHRRR!
WHRRR!
WHRRR!
ZOOMP!

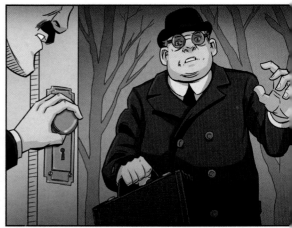

WELL THEN. VERY GOOD. MR. TESLA, IS IT?

YES

MUSTACHE A GIVEAWAY TO BE SURE.

MY NAME IS PETER MACKLEROY, ESQUIRE. NOW, MR. TESLA –

--DO YOU RECALL YOUR ORIGINAL WORKING AGREEMENT WITH MR. THOMAS EDISON, OWNER AND MANAGING DIRECTOR OF EDISON LABORATORIES,

THEIR SUBSIDIARIES AND ALL HOLDINGS, BOTH DOMESTIC AND EUROPEAN?

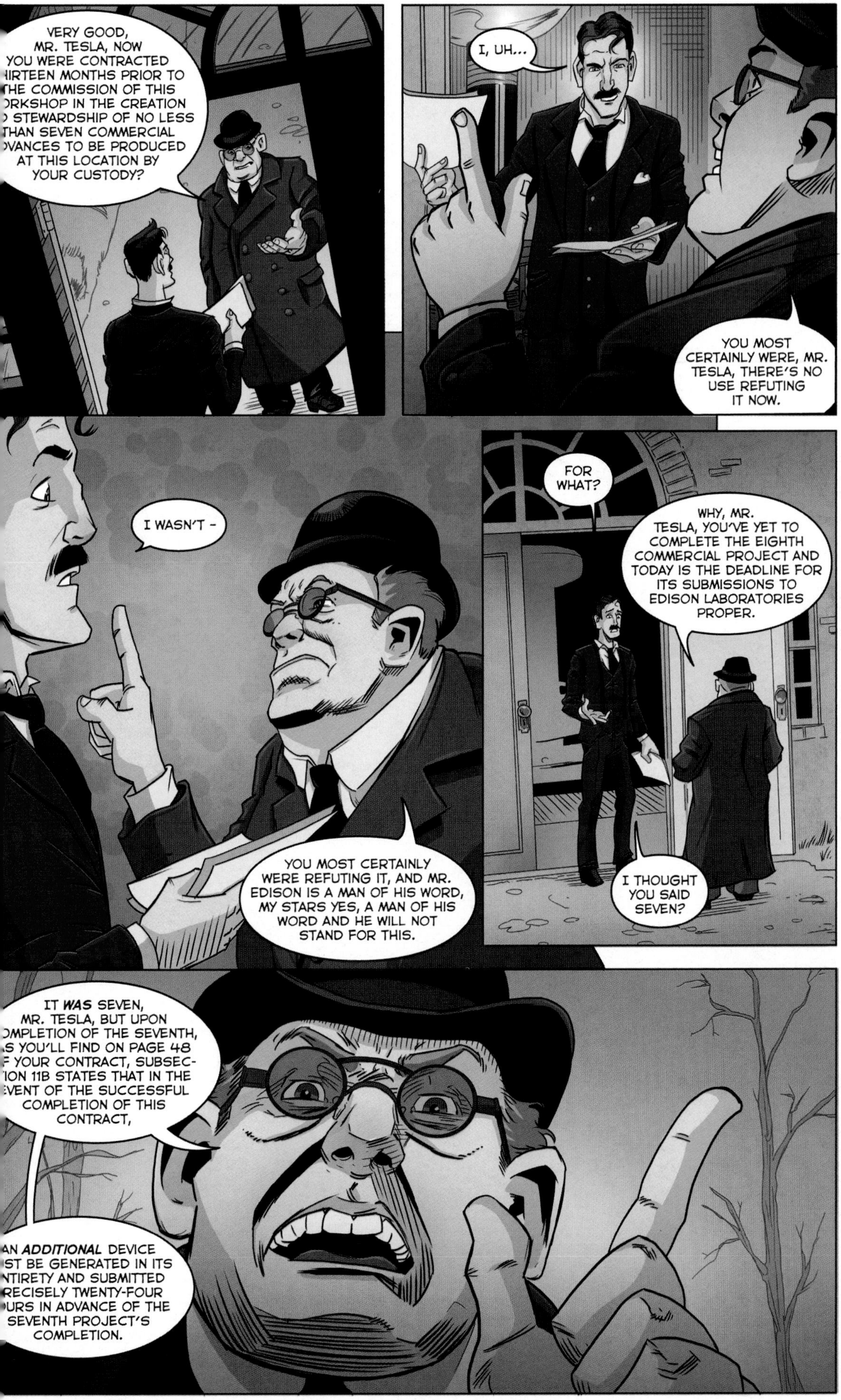
VERY GOOD, MR. TESLA, NOW YOU WERE CONTRACTED HIRTEEN MONTHS PRIOR TO THE COMMISSION OF THIS ORKSHOP IN THE CREATION STEWARDSHIP OF NO LESS THAN SEVEN COMMERCIAL VANCES TO BE PRODUCED AT THIS LOCATION BY YOUR CUSTODY?
I, UH...
YOU MOST CERTAINLY WERE, MR. TESLA, THERE'S NO USE REFUTING IT NOW.
I WASN'T -
YOU MOST CERTAINLY WERE REFUTING IT, AND MR. EDISON IS A MAN OF HIS WORD, MY STARS YES, A MAN OF HIS WORD AND HE WILL NOT STAND FOR THIS.
FOR WHAT?
WHY, MR. TESLA, YOU'VE YET TO COMPLETE THE EIGHTH COMMERCIAL PROJECT AND TODAY IS THE DEADLINE FOR ITS SUBMISSIONS TO EDISON LABORATORIES PROPER.
I THOUGHT YOU SAID SEVEN?
IT *WAS* SEVEN, MR. TESLA, BUT UPON OMPLETION OF THE SEVENTH, S YOU'LL FIND ON PAGE 48 F YOUR CONTRACT, SUBSEC- ION 11B STATES THAT IN THE EVENT OF THE SUCCESSFUL COMPLETION OF THIS CONTRACT,
AN ***ADDITIONAL*** DEVICE ST BE GENERATED IN ITS NTIRETY AND SUBMITTED RECISELY TWENTY-FOUR URS IN ADVANCE OF THE SEVENTH PROJECT'S COMPLETION.

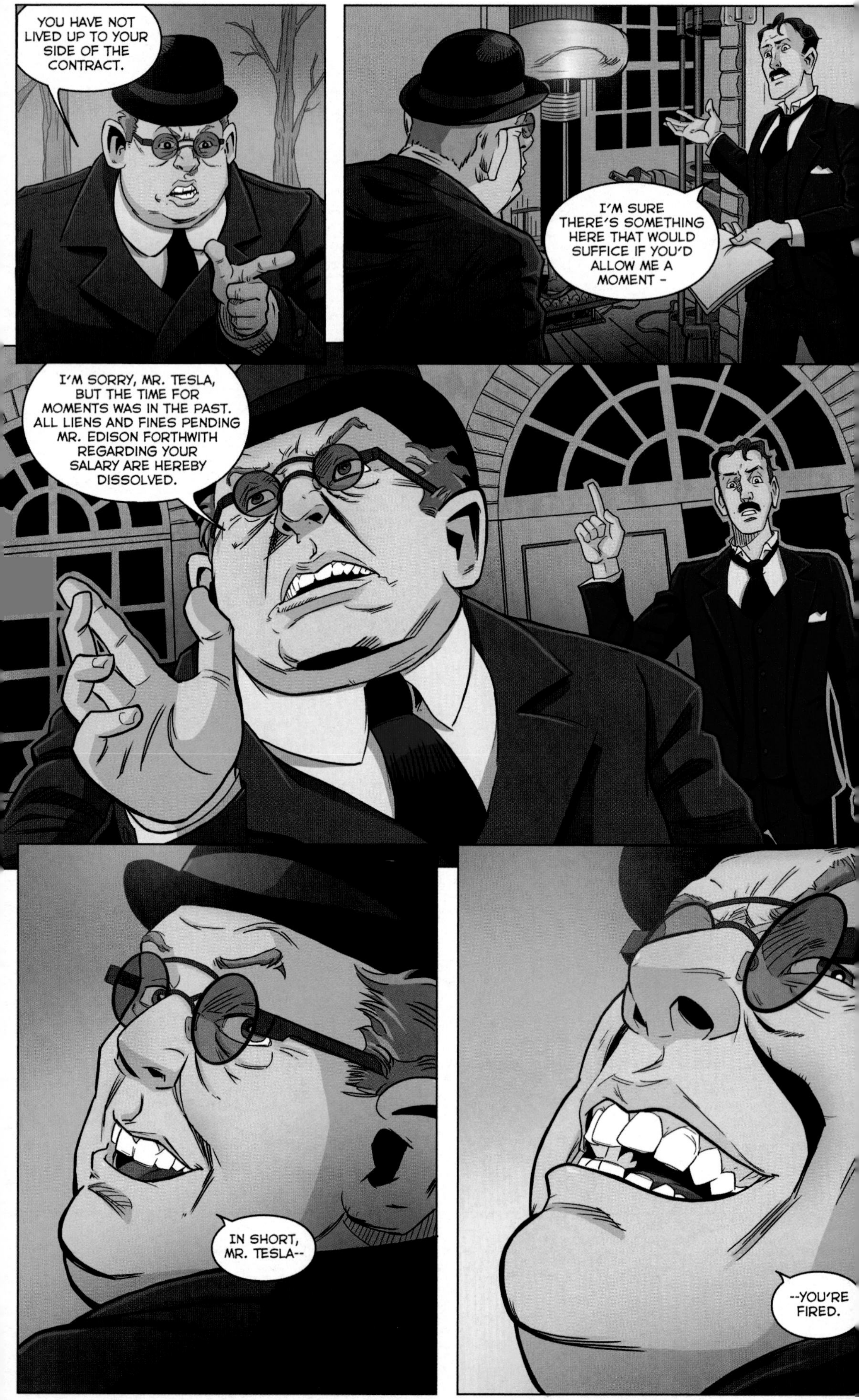
YOU HAVE NOT LIVED UP TO YOUR SIDE OF THE CONTRACT.
I'M SURE THERE'S SOMETHING HERE THAT WOULD SUFFICE IF YOU'D ALLOW ME A MOMENT -
I'M SORRY, MR. TESLA, BUT THE TIME FOR MOMENTS WAS IN THE PAST. ALL LIENS AND FINES PENDING MR. EDISON FORTHWITH REGARDING YOUR SALARY ARE HEREBY DISSOLVED.
IN SHORT, MR. TESLA--
--YOU'RE FIRED.

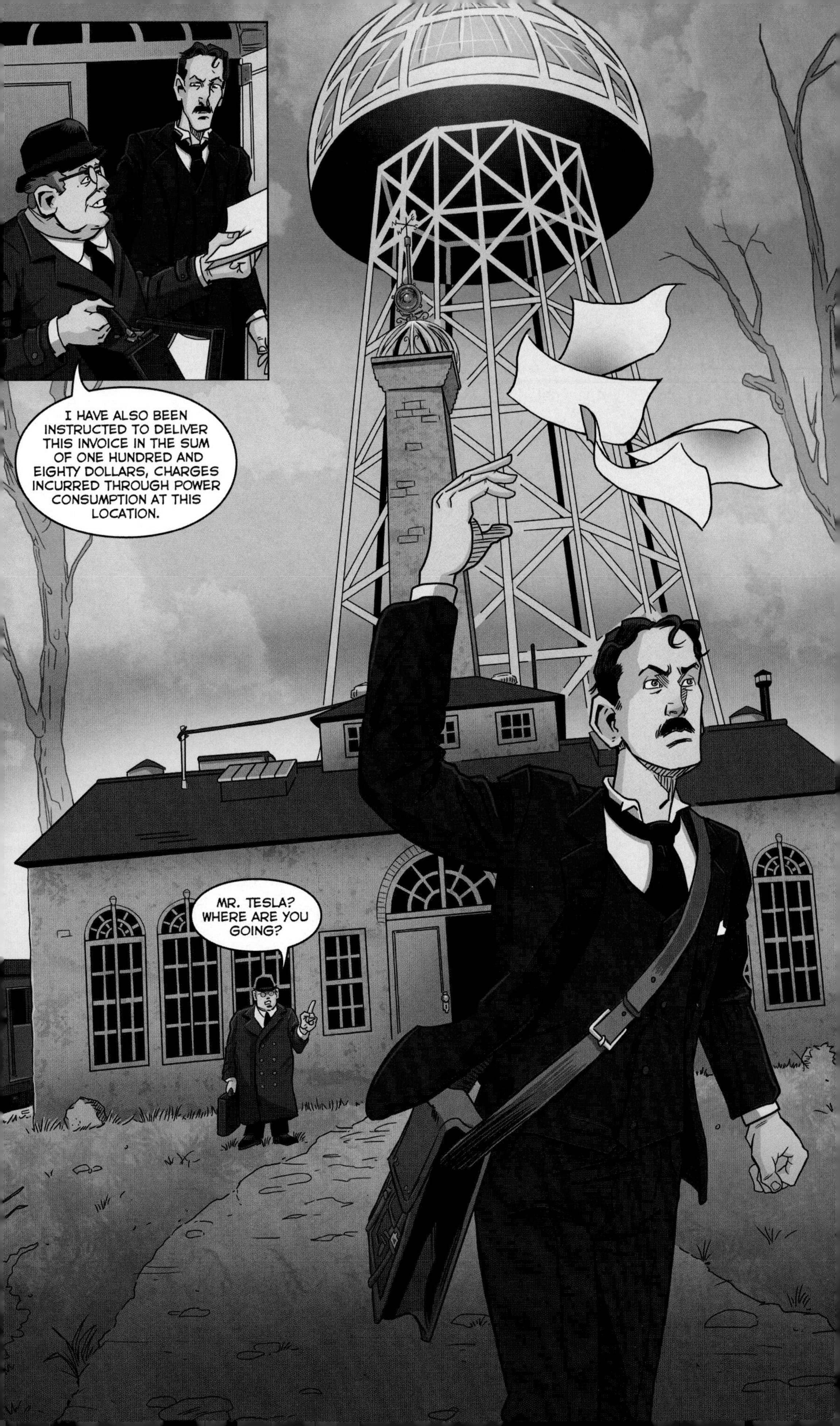
I HAVE ALSO BEEN INSTRUCTED TO DELIVER THIS INVOICE IN THE SUM OF ONE HUNDRED AND EIGHTY DOLLARS, CHARGES INCURRED THROUGH POWER CONSUMPTION AT THIS LOCATION.
MR. TESLA? WHERE ARE YOU GOING?

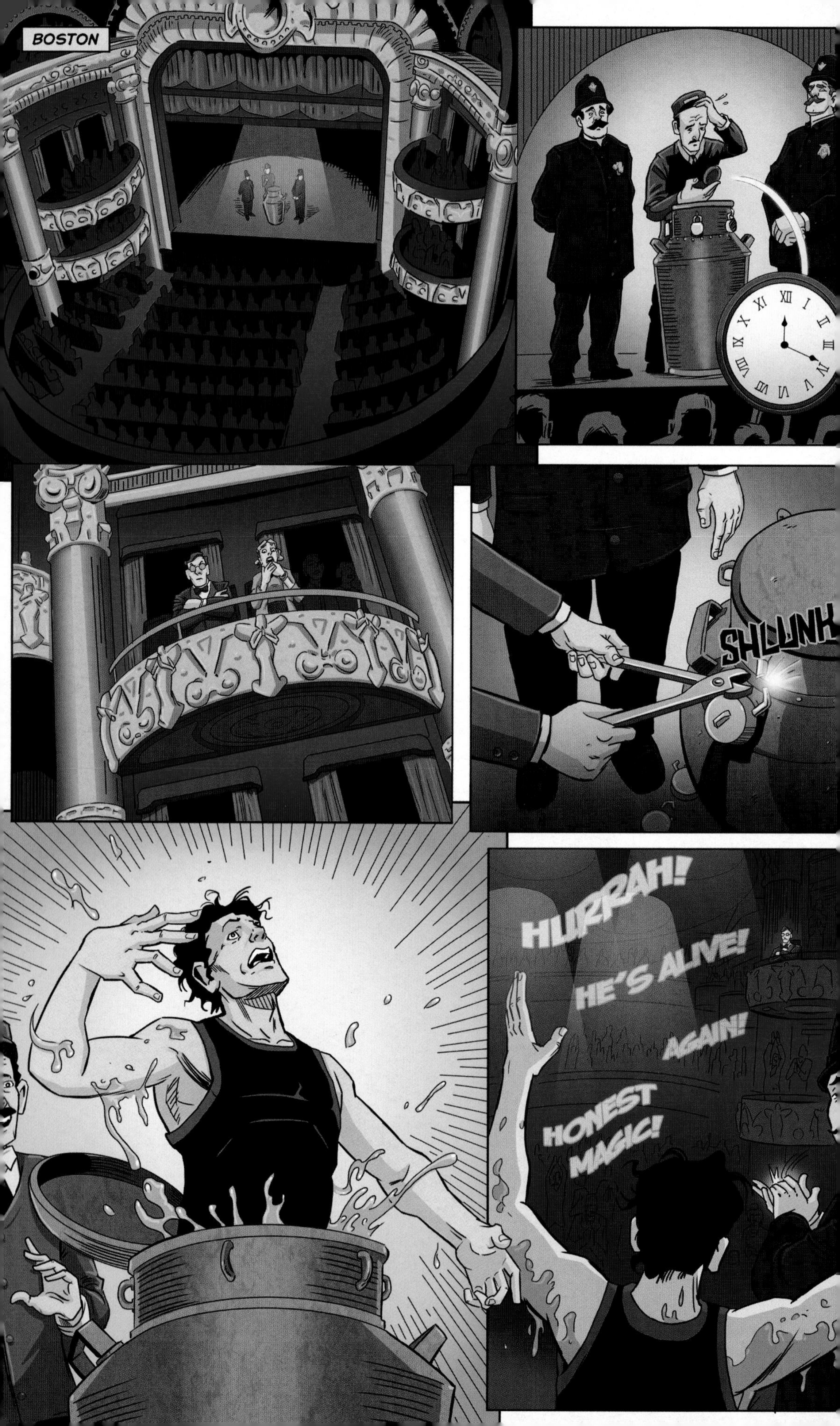
BOSTON
SHLUNK
HURRAH!
HE'S ALIVE!
AGAIN!
HONEST MAGIC!

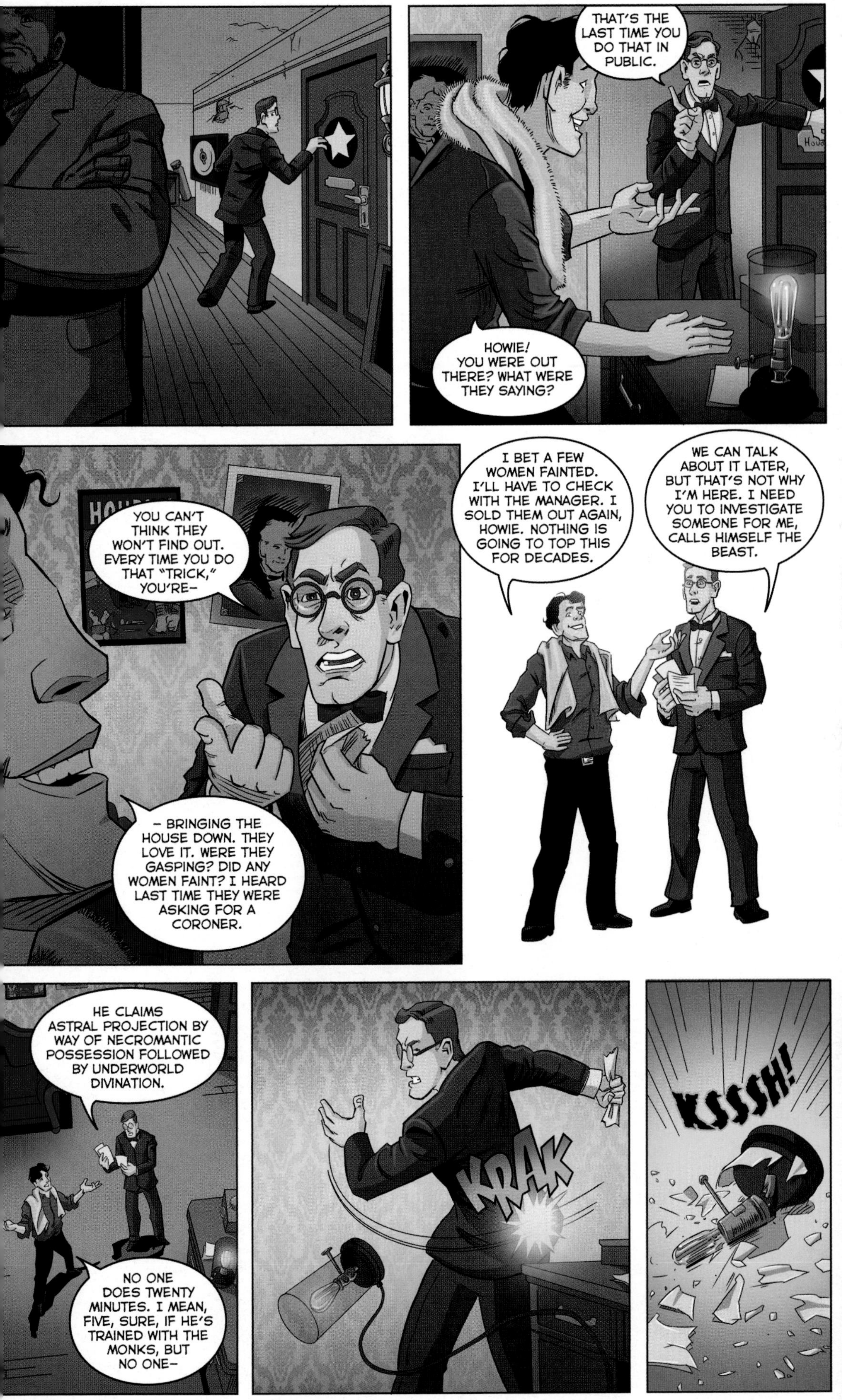
THAT'S THE LAST TIME YOU DO THAT IN PUBLIC.
HOWIE! YOU WERE OUT THERE? WHAT WERE THEY SAYING?
YOU CAN'T THINK THEY WON'T FIND OUT. EVERY TIME YOU DO THAT "TRICK," YOU'RE–
– BRINGING THE HOUSE DOWN. THEY LOVE IT. WERE THEY GASPING? DID ANY WOMEN FAINT? I HEARD LAST TIME THEY WERE ASKING FOR A CORONER.
I BET A FEW WOMEN FAINTED. I'LL HAVE TO CHECK WITH THE MANAGER. I SOLD THEM OUT AGAIN, HOWIE. NOTHING IS GOING TO TOP THIS FOR DECADES.
WE CAN TALK ABOUT IT LATER, BUT THAT'S NOT WHY I'M HERE. I NEED YOU TO INVESTIGATE SOMEONE FOR ME, CALLS HIMSELF THE BEAST.
HE CLAIMS ASTRAL PROJECTION BY WAY OF NECROMANTIC POSSESSION FOLLOWED BY UNDERWORLD DIVINATION.
NO ONE DOES TWENTY MINUTES. I MEAN, FIVE, SURE, IF HE'S TRAINED WITH THE MONKS, BUT NO ONE–
KRAK
KSSSH!

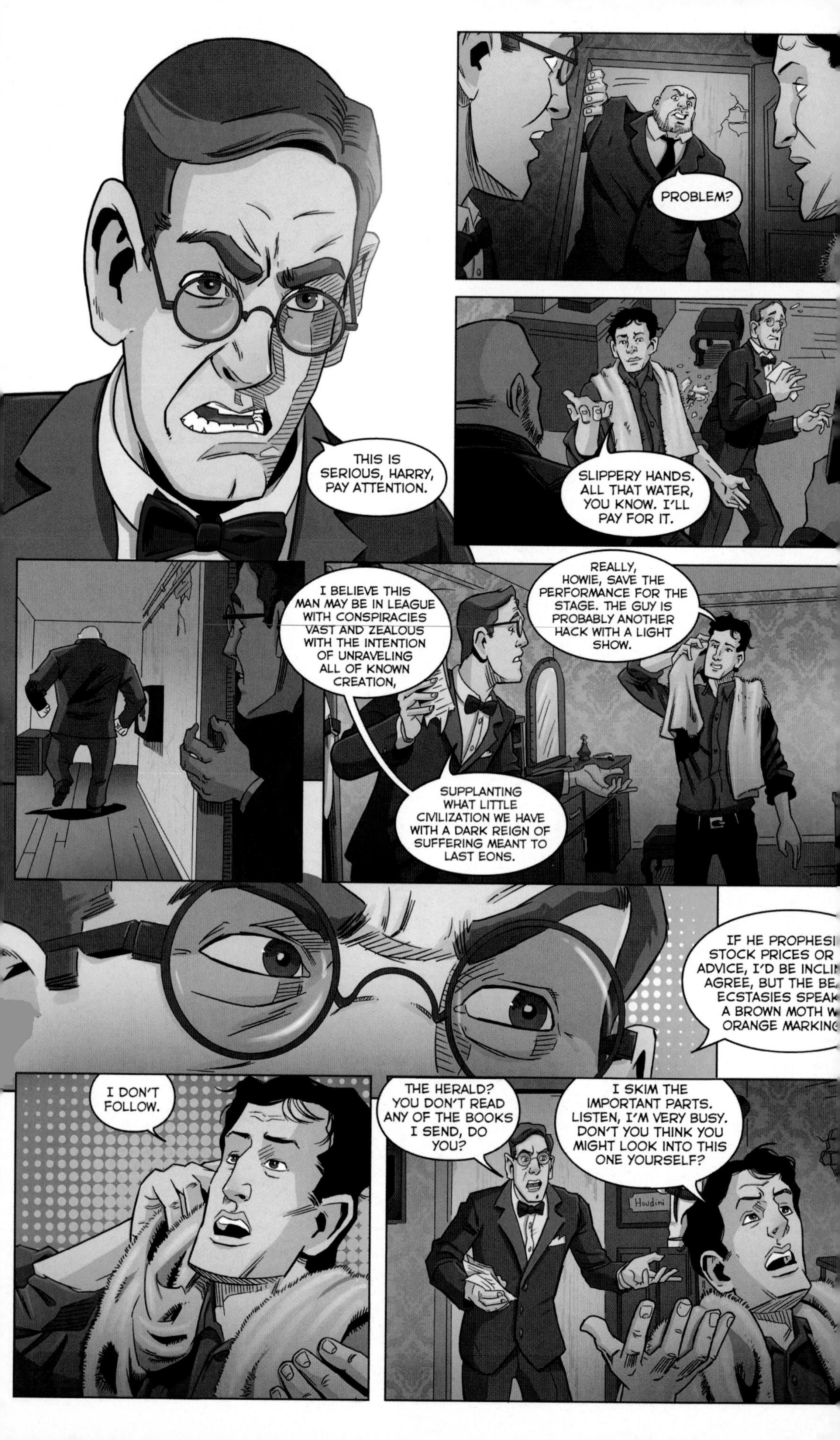
THIS IS SERIOUS, HARRY, PAY ATTENTION.
PROBLEM?
SLIPPERY HANDS. ALL THAT WATER, YOU KNOW. I'LL PAY FOR IT.
I BELIEVE THIS MAN MAY BE IN LEAGUE WITH CONSPIRACIES VAST AND ZEALOUS WITH THE INTENTION OF UNRAVELING ALL OF KNOWN CREATION,
SUPPLANTING WHAT LITTLE CIVILIZATION WE HAVE WITH A DARK REIGN OF SUFFERING MEANT TO LAST EONS.
REALLY, HOWIE, SAVE THE PERFORMANCE FOR THE STAGE. THE GUY IS PROBABLY ANOTHER HACK WITH A LIGHT SHOW.
IF HE PROPHESI STOCK PRICES OR ADVICE, I'D BE INCLI AGREE, BUT THE BE ECSTASIES SPEAK A BROWN MOTH W ORANGE MARKING
I DON'T FOLLOW.
THE HERALD? YOU DON'T READ ANY OF THE BOOKS I SEND, DO YOU?
I SKIM THE IMPORTANT PARTS. LISTEN, I'M VERY BUSY. DON'T YOU THINK YOU MIGHT LOOK INTO THIS ONE YOURSELF?
Houdini

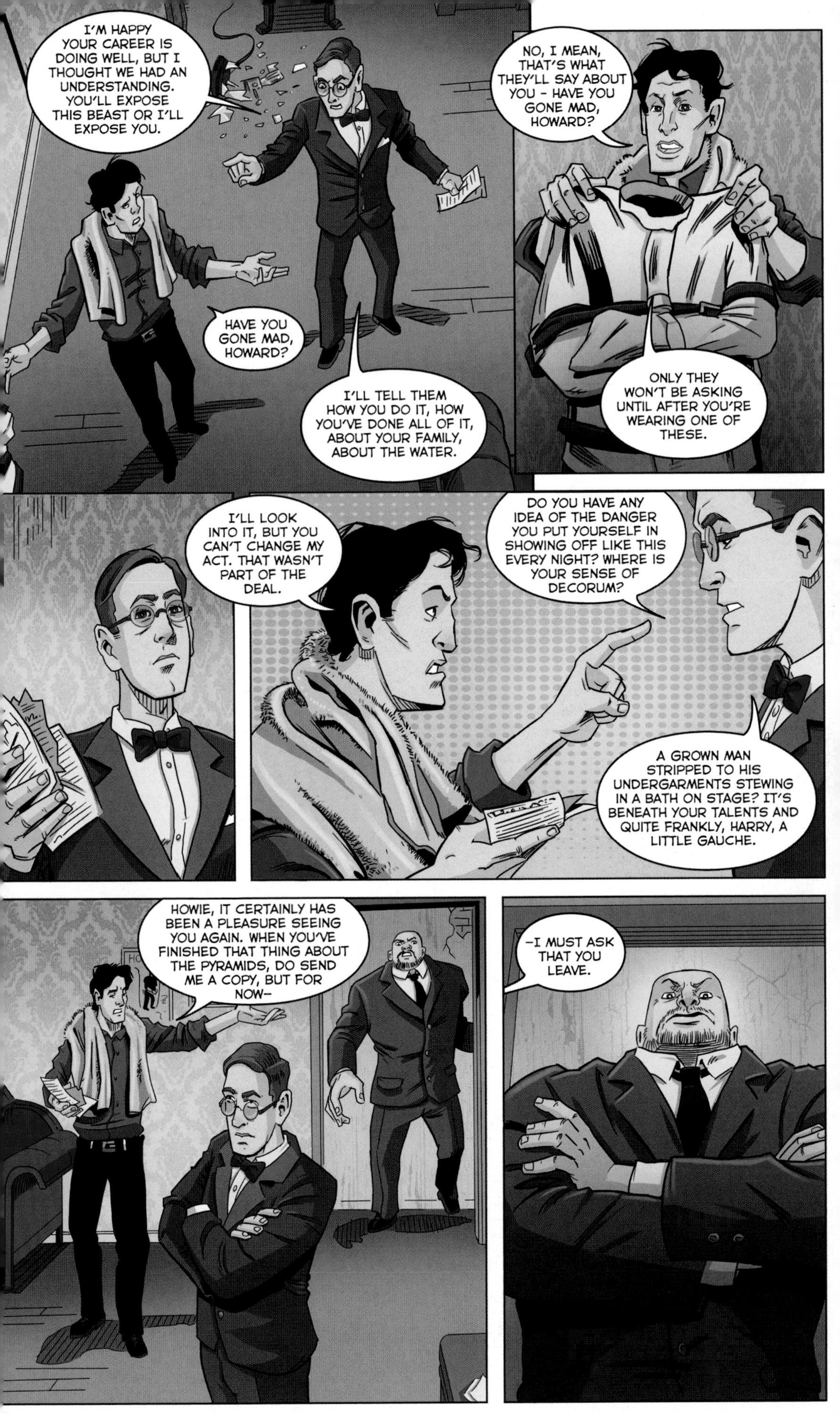
I'M HAPPY YOUR CAREER IS DOING WELL, BUT I THOUGHT WE HAD AN UNDERSTANDING. YOU'LL EXPOSE THIS BEAST OR I'LL EXPOSE YOU.
HAVE YOU GONE MAD, HOWARD?
I'LL TELL THEM HOW YOU DO IT, HOW YOU'VE DONE ALL OF IT, ABOUT YOUR FAMILY, ABOUT THE WATER.
NO, I MEAN, THAT'S WHAT THEY'LL SAY ABOUT YOU - HAVE YOU GONE MAD, HOWARD?
ONLY THEY WON'T BE ASKING UNTIL AFTER YOU'RE WEARING ONE OF THESE.
I'LL LOOK INTO IT, BUT YOU CAN'T CHANGE MY ACT. THAT WASN'T PART OF THE DEAL.
DO YOU HAVE ANY IDEA OF THE DANGER YOU PUT YOURSELF IN SHOWING OFF LIKE THIS EVERY NIGHT? WHERE IS YOUR SENSE OF DECORUM?
A GROWN MAN STRIPPED TO HIS UNDERGARMENTS STEWING IN A BATH ON STAGE? IT'S BENEATH YOUR TALENTS AND QUITE FRANKLY, HARRY, A LITTLE GAUCHE.
HOWIE, IT CERTAINLY HAS BEEN A PLEASURE SEEING YOU AGAIN. WHEN YOU'VE FINISHED THAT THING ABOUT THE PYRAMIDS, DO SEND ME A COPY, BUT FOR NOW–
–I MUST ASK THAT YOU LEAVE.

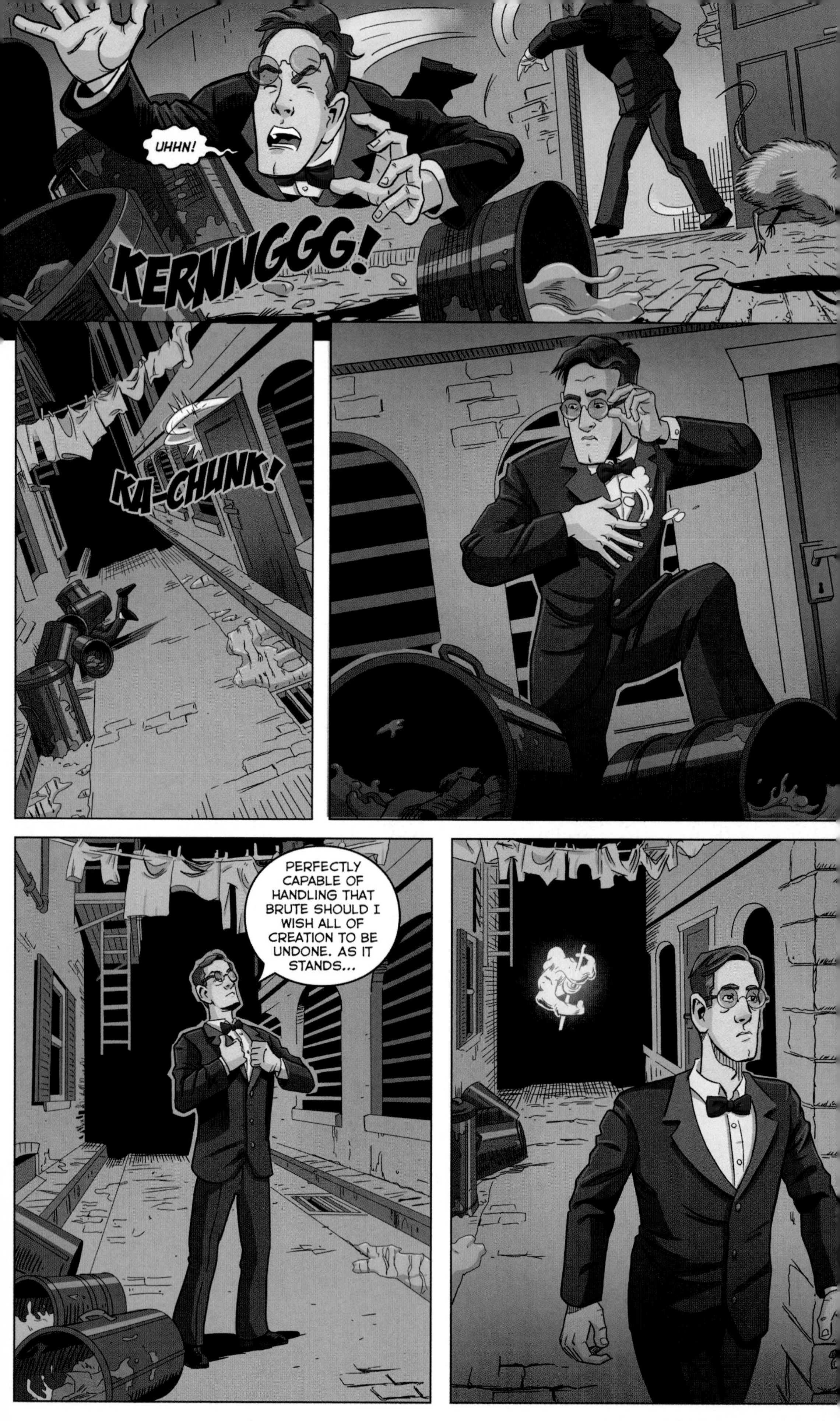
UHHN!
KERNNGGG!
KA-CHUNK!
PERFECTLY CAPABLE OF HANDLING THAT BRUTE SHOULD I WISH ALL OF CREATION TO BE UNDONE. AS IT STANDS...

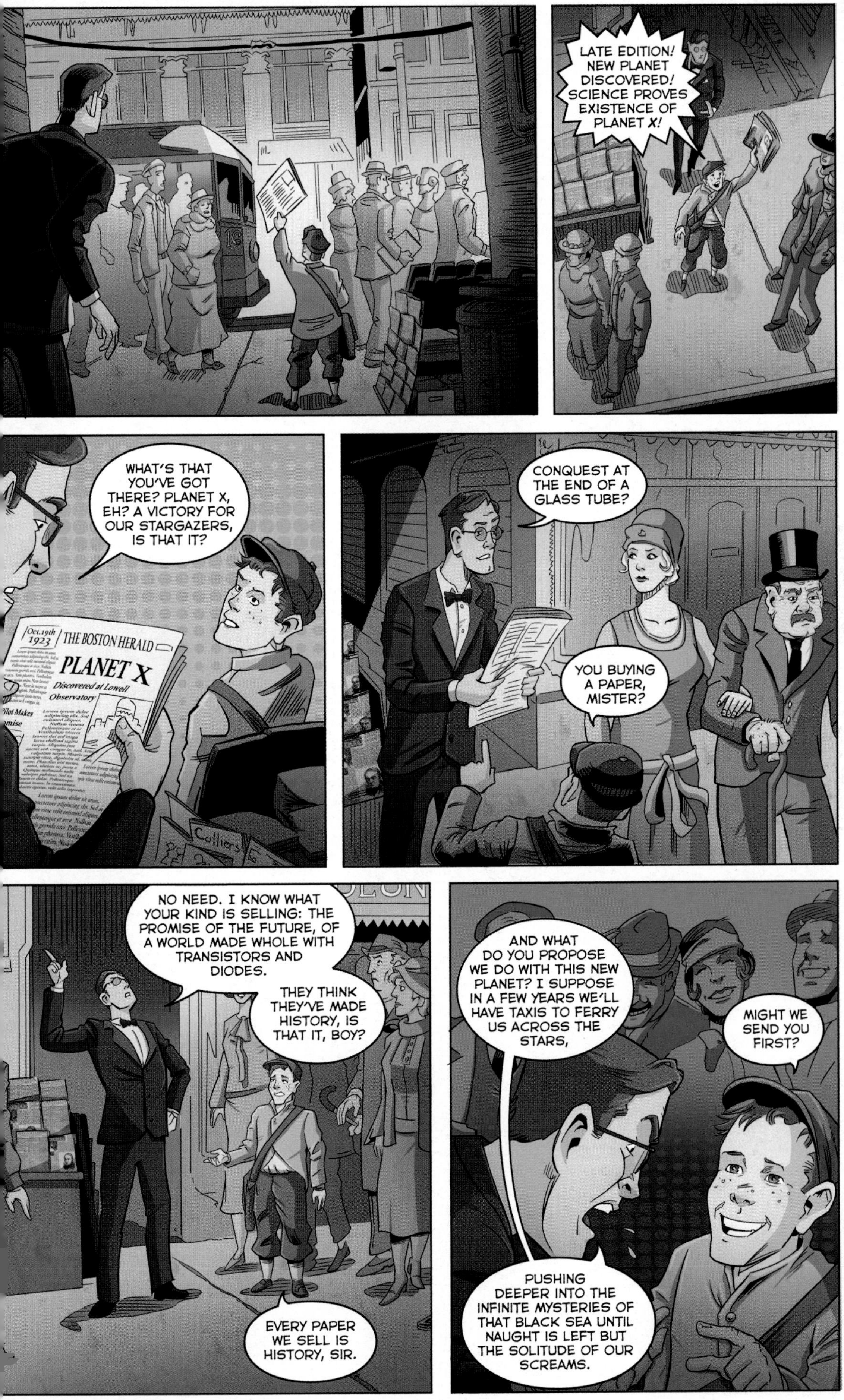
LATE EDITION! NEW PLANET DISCOVERED! SCIENCE PROVES EXISTENCE OF PLANET X!
WHAT'S THAT YOU'VE GOT THERE? PLANET X, EH? A VICTORY FOR OUR STARGAZERS, IS THAT IT?
Oct. 19th 1923
THE BOSTON HERALD
PLANET X
Discovered at Lowell Observatory
Colliers
CONQUEST AT THE END OF A GLASS TUBE?
YOU BUYING A PAPER, MISTER?
NO NEED. I KNOW WHAT YOUR KIND IS SELLING: THE PROMISE OF THE FUTURE, OF A WORLD MADE WHOLE WITH TRANSISTORS AND DIODES.
THEY THINK THEY'VE MADE HISTORY, IS THAT IT, BOY?
EVERY PAPER WE SELL IS HISTORY, SIR.
AND WHAT DO YOU PROPOSE WE DO WITH THIS NEW PLANET? I SUPPOSE IN A FEW YEARS WE'LL HAVE TAXIS TO FERRY US ACROSS THE STARS,
PUSHING DEEPER INTO THE INFINITE MYSTERIES OF THAT BLACK SEA UNTIL NAUGHT IS LEFT BUT THE SOLITUDE OF OUR SCREAMS.
MIGHT WE SEND YOU FIRST?

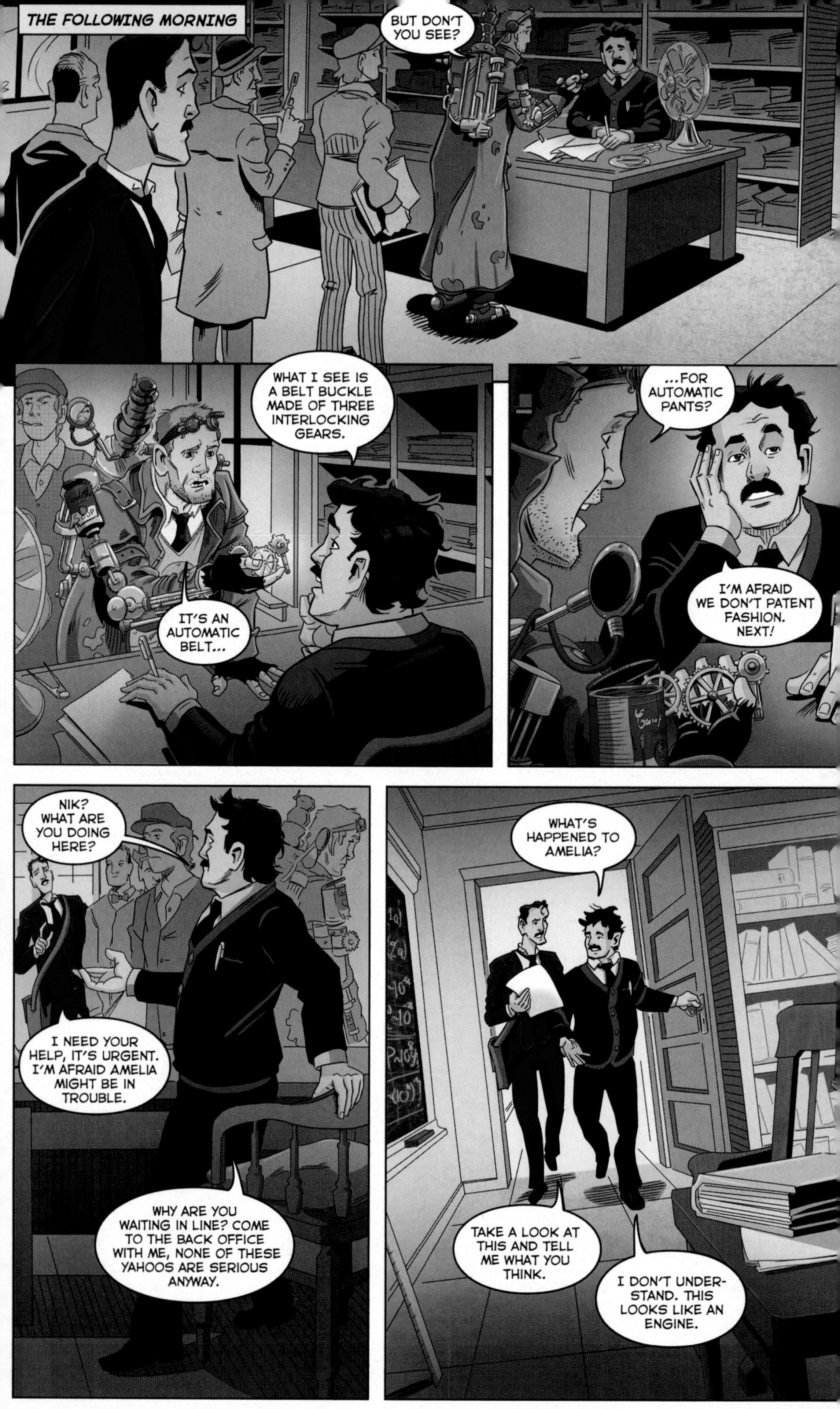
THE FOLLOWING MORNING
BUT DON'T YOU SEE?
WHAT I SEE IS A BELT BUCKLE MADE OF THREE INTERLOCKING GEARS.
IT'S AN AUTOMATIC BELT...
...FOR AUTOMATIC PANTS?
I'M AFRAID WE DON'T PATENT FASHION. NEXT!
NIK? WHAT ARE YOU DOING HERE?
I NEED YOUR HELP, IT'S URGENT. I'M AFRAID AMELIA MIGHT BE IN TROUBLE.
WHY ARE YOU WAITING IN LINE? COME TO THE BACK OFFICE WITH ME, NONE OF THESE YAHOOS ARE SERIOUS ANYWAY.
WHAT'S HAPPENED TO AMELIA?
TAKE A LOOK AT THIS AND TELL ME WHAT YOU THINK.
I DON'T UNDERSTAND. THIS LOOKS LIKE AN ENGINE.

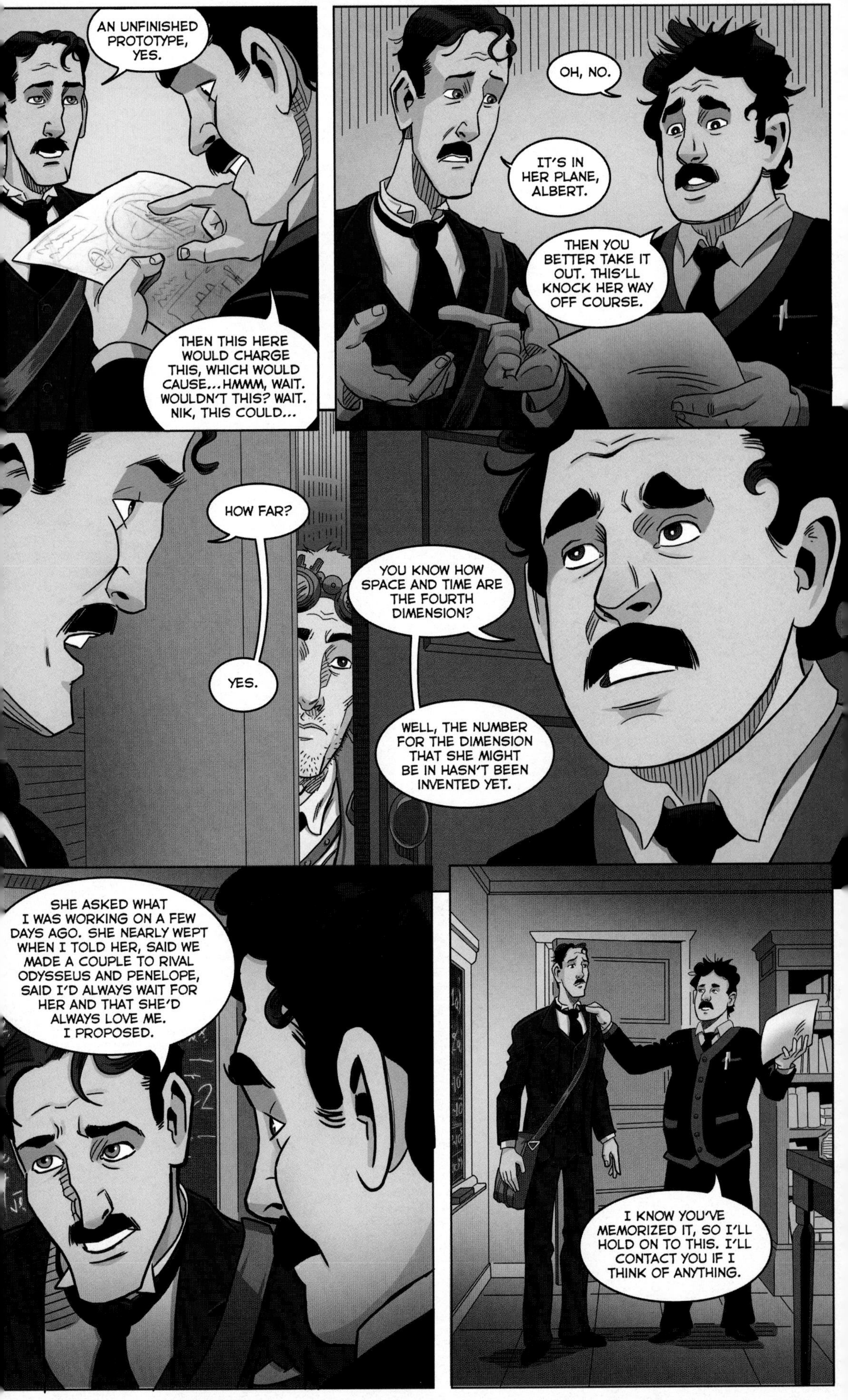
AN UNFINISHED PROTOTYPE, YES.
THEN THIS HERE WOULD CHARGE THIS, WHICH WOULD CAUSE...HMMM, WAIT. WOULDN'T THIS? WAIT. NIK, THIS COULD...
OH, NO.
IT'S IN HER PLANE, ALBERT.
THEN YOU BETTER TAKE IT OUT. THIS'LL KNOCK HER WAY OFF COURSE.
HOW FAR?
YES.
YOU KNOW HOW SPACE AND TIME ARE THE FOURTH DIMENSION?
WELL, THE NUMBER FOR THE DIMENSION THAT SHE MIGHT BE IN HASN'T BEEN INVENTED YET.
SHE ASKED WHAT I WAS WORKING ON A FEW DAYS AGO. SHE NEARLY WEPT WHEN I TOLD HER, SAID WE MADE A COUPLE TO RIVAL ODYSSEUS AND PENELOPE, SAID I'D ALWAYS WAIT FOR HER AND THAT SHE'D ALWAYS LOVE ME. I PROPOSED.
I KNOW YOU'VE MEMORIZED IT, SO I'LL HOLD ON TO THIS. I'LL CONTACT YOU IF I THINK OF ANYTHING.

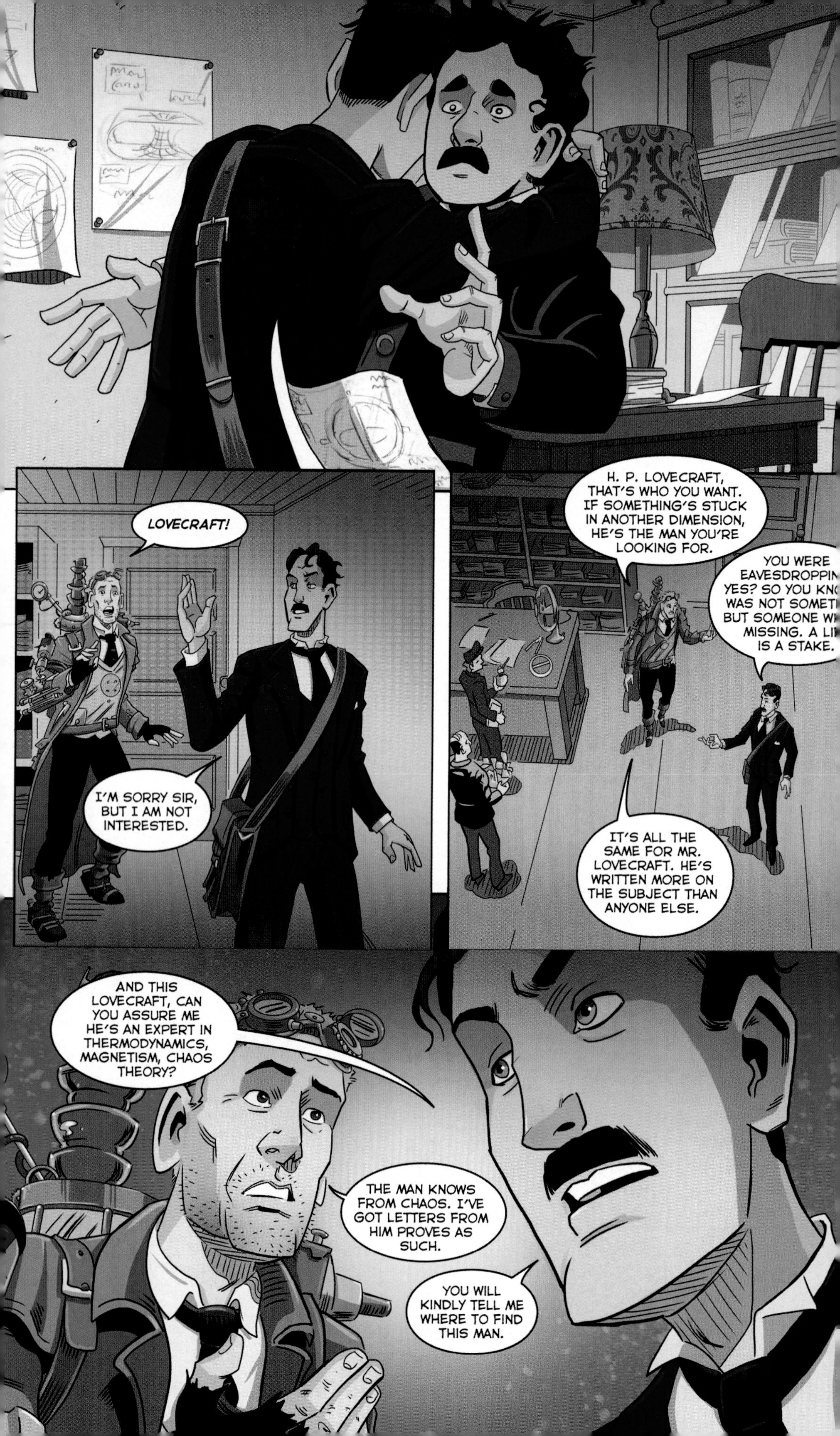
LOVECRAFT!
I'M SORRY SIR, BUT I AM NOT INTERESTED.
H. P. LOVECRAFT, THAT'S WHO YOU WANT. IF SOMETHING'S STUCK IN ANOTHER DIMENSION, HE'S THE MAN YOU'RE LOOKING FOR.
YOU WERE EAVESDROPPIN YES? SO YOU KNO WAS NOT SOMET BUT SOMEONE W MISSING. A LI IS A STAKE.
IT'S ALL THE SAME FOR MR. LOVECRAFT. HE'S WRITTEN MORE ON THE SUBJECT THAN ANYONE ELSE.
AND THIS LOVECRAFT, CAN YOU ASSURE ME HE'S AN EXPERT IN THERMODYNAMICS, MAGNETISM, CHAOS THEORY?
THE MAN KNOWS FROM CHAOS. I'VE GOT LETTERS FROM HIM PROVES AS SUCH.
YOU WILL KINDLY TELL ME WHERE TO FIND THIS MAN.

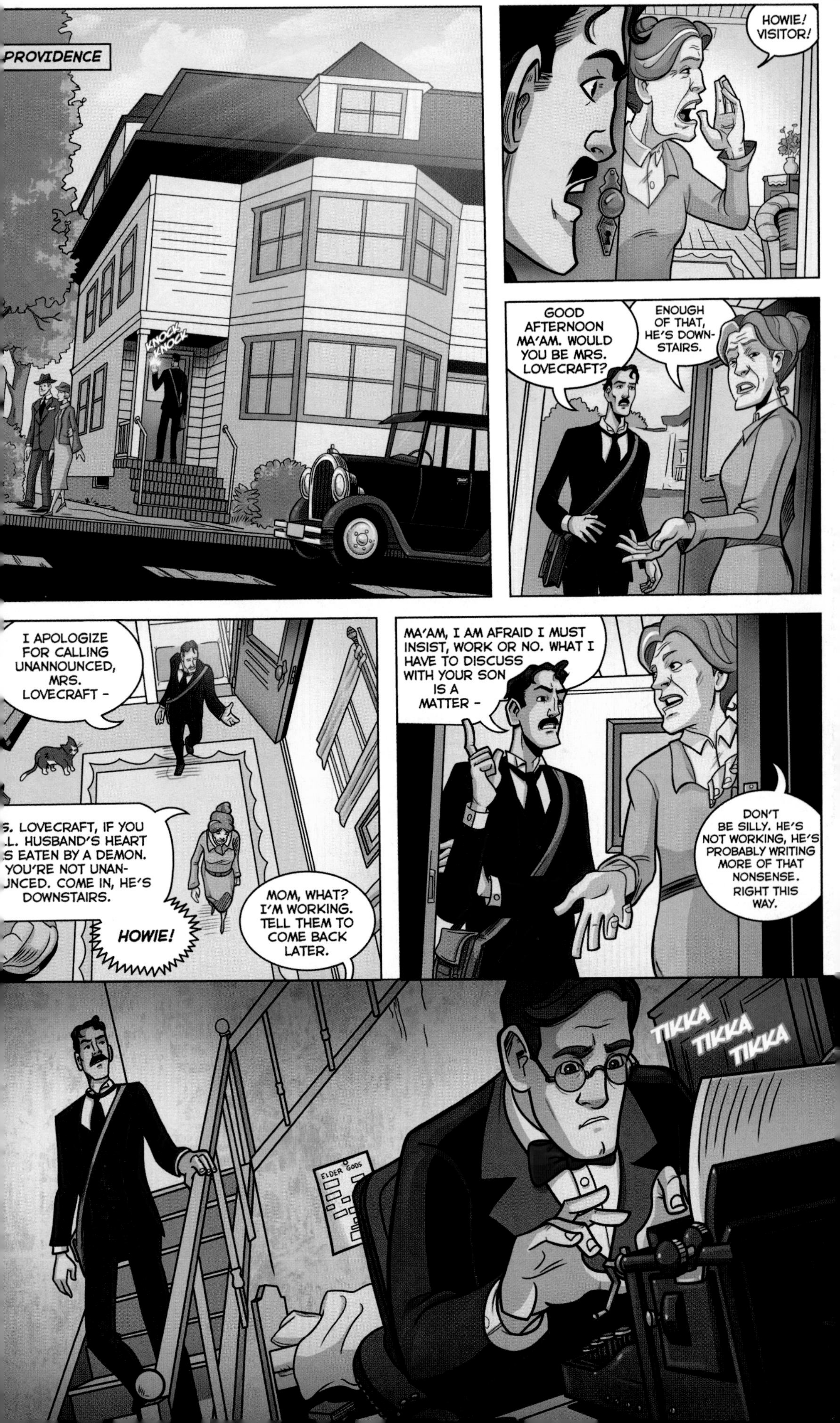
PROVIDENCE
KNOCK KNOCK
HOWIE! VISITOR!
GOOD AFTERNOON MA'AM. WOULD YOU BE MRS. LOVECRAFT?
ENOUGH OF THAT, HE'S DOWN-STAIRS.
I APOLOGIZE FOR CALLING UNANNOUNCED, MRS. LOVECRAFT -
S. LOVECRAFT, IF YOU .L. HUSBAND'S HEART S EATEN BY A DEMON. YOU'RE NOT UNAN- UNCED. COME IN, HE'S DOWNSTAIRS.
HOWIE!
MOM, WHAT? I'M WORKING. TELL THEM TO COME BACK LATER.
MA'AM, I AM AFRAID I MUST INSIST, WORK OR NO. WHAT I HAVE TO DISCUSS WITH YOUR SON IS A MATTER -
DON'T BE SILLY. HE'S NOT WORKING, HE'S PROBABLY WRITING MORE OF THAT NONSENSE. RIGHT THIS WAY.
TIKKA TIKKA TIKKA
ELDER GODS

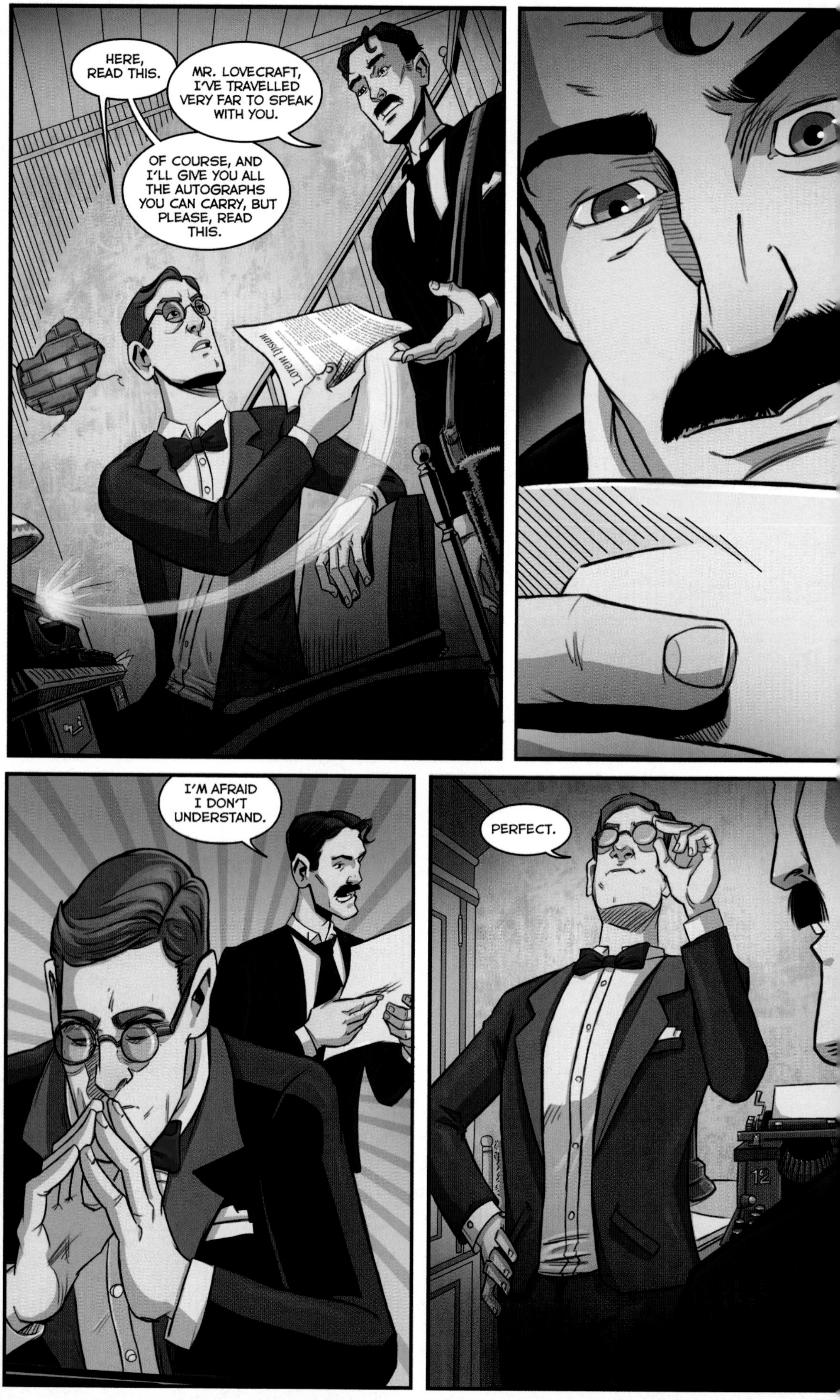
HERE, READ THIS.
MR. LOVECRAFT, I'VE TRAVELLED VERY FAR TO SPEAK WITH YOU.
OF COURSE, AND I'LL GIVE YOU ALL THE AUTOGRAPHS YOU CAN CARRY, BUT PLEASE, READ THIS.
I'M AFRAID I DON'T UNDERSTAND.
PERFECT.

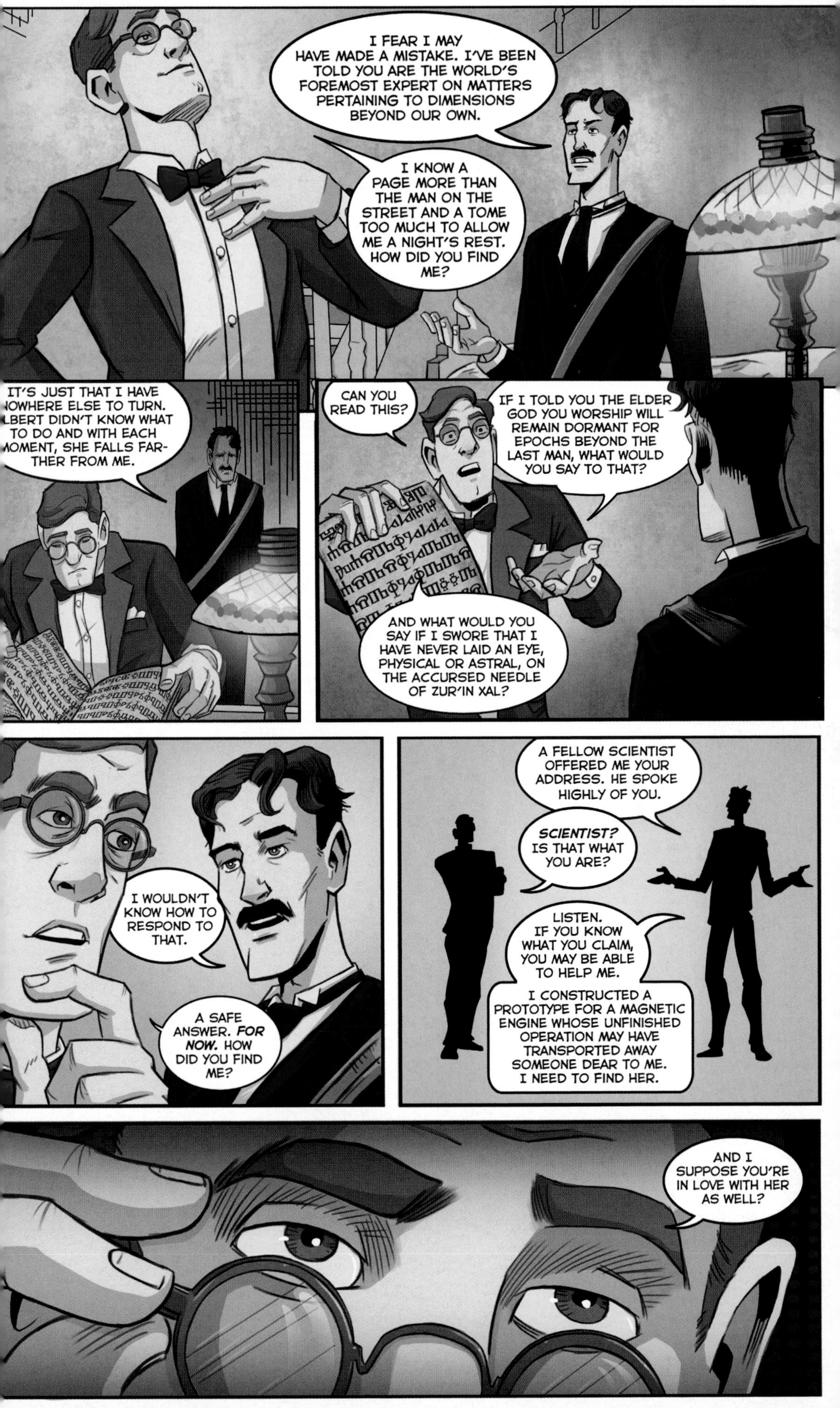
I FEAR I MAY HAVE MADE A MISTAKE. I'VE BEEN TOLD YOU ARE THE WORLD'S FOREMOST EXPERT ON MATTERS PERTAINING TO DIMENSIONS BEYOND OUR OWN.
I KNOW A PAGE MORE THAN THE MAN ON THE STREET AND A TOME TOO MUCH TO ALLOW ME A NIGHT'S REST. HOW DID YOU FIND ME?
IT'S JUST THAT I HAVE OWHERE ELSE TO TURN. LBERT DIDN'T KNOW WHAT TO DO AND WITH EACH OMENT, SHE FALLS FARTHER FROM ME.
CAN YOU READ THIS?
IF I TOLD YOU THE ELDER GOD YOU WORSHIP WILL REMAIN DORMANT FOR EPOCHS BEYOND THE LAST MAN, WHAT WOULD YOU SAY TO THAT?
AND WHAT WOULD YOU SAY IF I SWORE THAT I HAVE NEVER LAID AN EYE, PHYSICAL OR ASTRAL, ON THE ACCURSED NEEDLE OF ZUR'IN XAL?
I WOULDN'T KNOW HOW TO RESPOND TO THAT.
A SAFE ANSWER. *FOR NOW.* HOW DID YOU FIND ME?
A FELLOW SCIENTIST OFFERED ME YOUR ADDRESS. HE SPOKE HIGHLY OF YOU.
SCIENTIST? IS THAT WHAT YOU ARE?
LISTEN. IF YOU KNOW WHAT YOU CLAIM, YOU MAY BE ABLE TO HELP ME.
I CONSTRUCTED A PROTOTYPE FOR A MAGNETIC ENGINE WHOSE UNFINISHED OPERATION MAY HAVE TRANSPORTED AWAY SOMEONE DEAR TO ME. I NEED TO FIND HER.
AND I SUPPOSE YOU'RE IN LOVE WITH HER AS WELL?

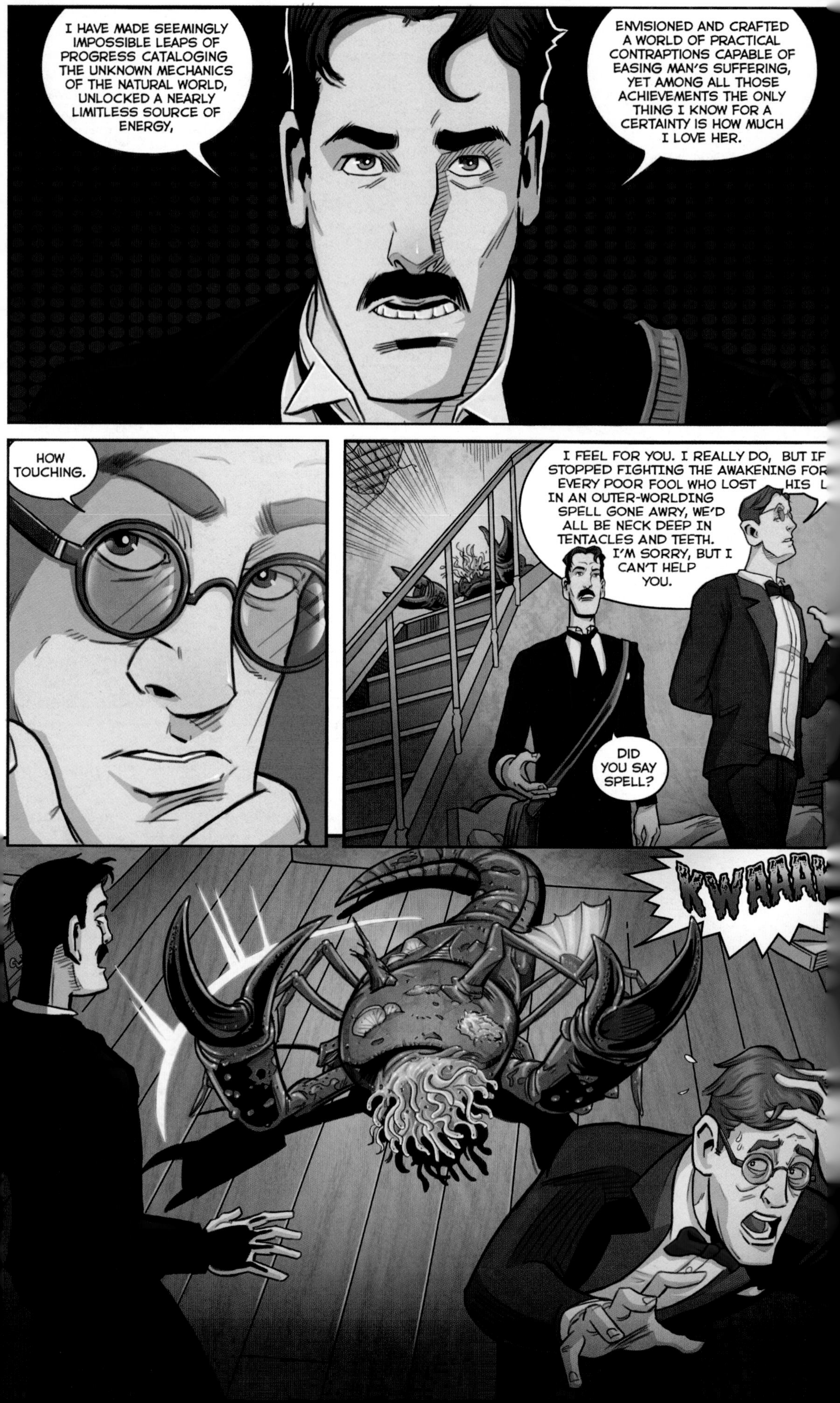
I HAVE MADE SEEMINGLY IMPOSSIBLE LEAPS OF PROGRESS CATALOGING THE UNKNOWN MECHANICS OF THE NATURAL WORLD, UNLOCKED A NEARLY LIMITLESS SOURCE OF ENERGY,
ENVISIONED AND CRAFTED A WORLD OF PRACTICAL CONTRAPTIONS CAPABLE OF EASING MAN'S SUFFERING, YET AMONG ALL THOSE ACHIEVEMENTS THE ONLY THING I KNOW FOR A CERTAINTY IS HOW MUCH I LOVE HER.
HOW TOUCHING.
I FEEL FOR YOU. I REALLY DO, BUT IF STOPPED FIGHTING THE AWAKENING FOR EVERY POOR FOOL WHO LOST HIS L
IN AN OUTER-WORLDING SPELL GONE AWRY, WE'D ALL BE NECK DEEP IN TENTACLES AND TEETH.
I'M SORRY, BUT I CAN'T HELP YOU.
DID YOU SAY SPELL?
KWAAA

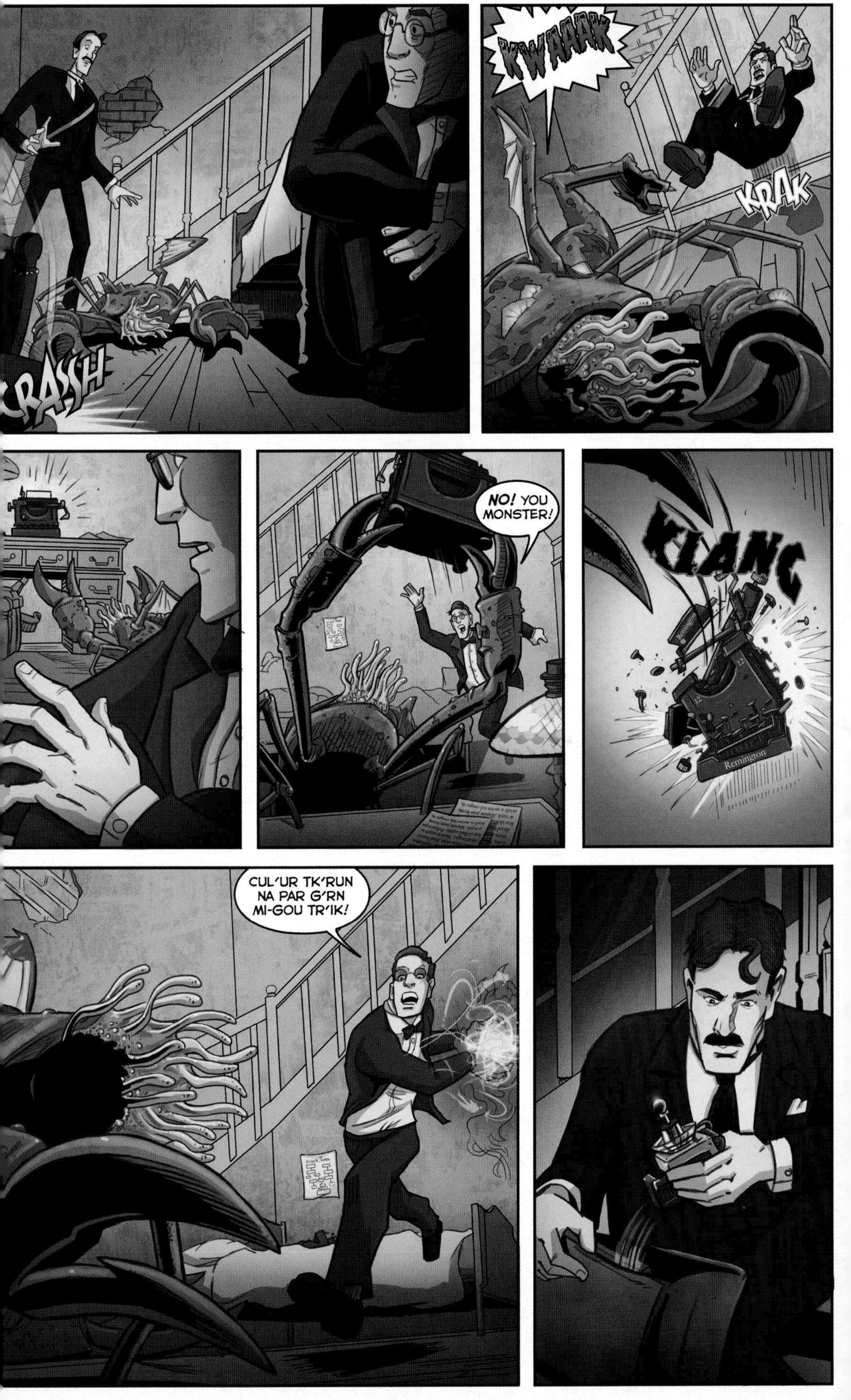
CRASH
KWAAAK
KRAK
NO! YOU MONSTER!
KLANG
Remington
Remington
CUL'UR TK'RUN NA PAR G'RN MI-GOU TR'IK!

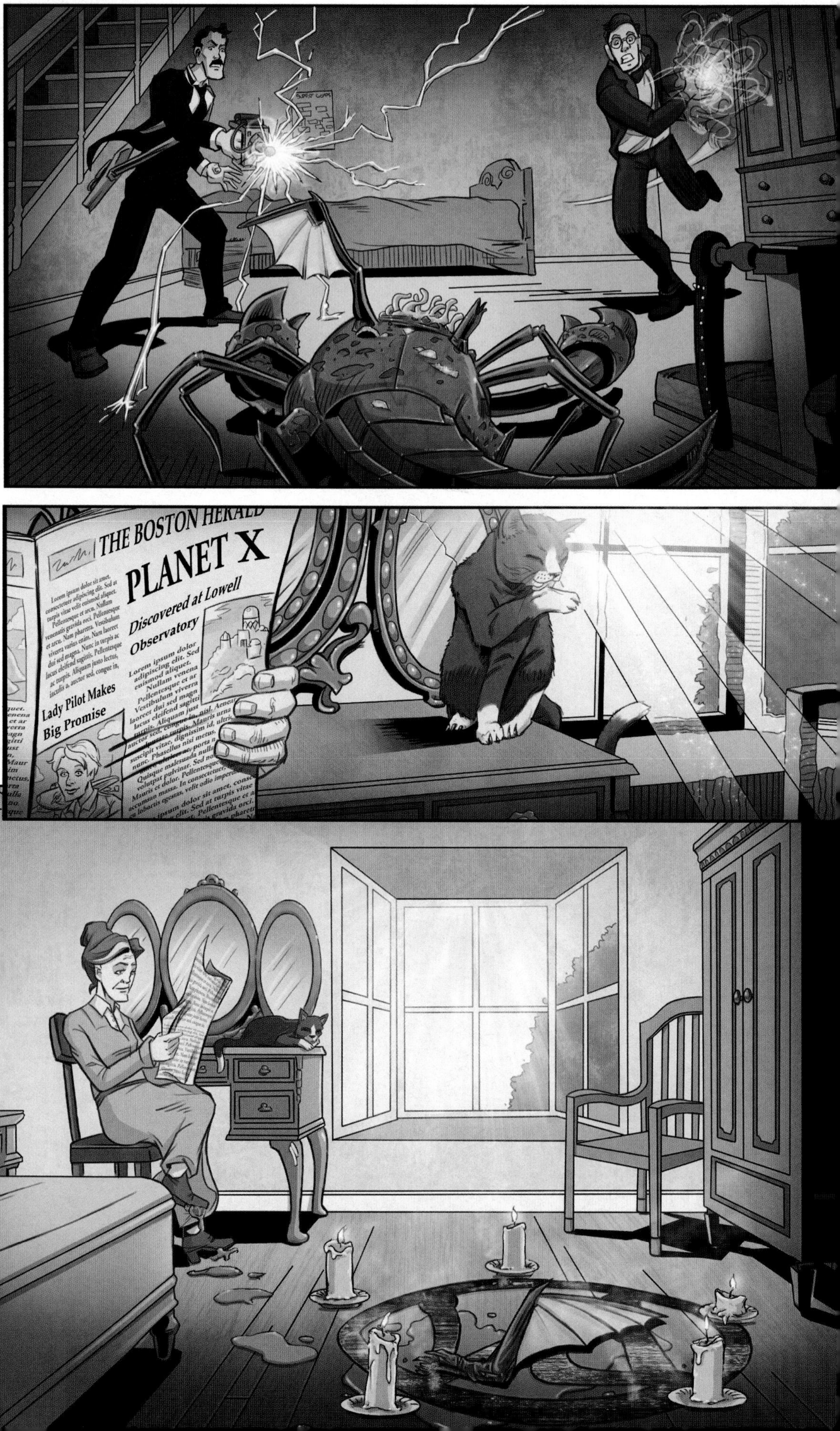
THE BOSTON HERALD
PLANET X
Discovered at Lowell Observatory
Lady Pilot Makes Big Promise

ᴁERALD
Lovecraft & Tesla

History in the Making
Issue 1 of 3

"History doesn't repeat itself, but it does rhyme."
- Mark Twain

Written by **John Reilly**

Pencils by **Tom Rogers**

Ink, Color, Letters by **Dexter Weeks**

Logo Design and Pg. 17 Inks by **Michelle Nikolajevic**

Variant Cover by **Colin Dyer**

on Lab Comics

her - Bryan Seaton   President - Kevin Freeman   Creative Director - Dave Dwonch

-in-Chief - Shawn Gabborin   Co-Directors of Marketing - Jamal Igle & Kelly Dale

Media Director - Jim Dietz   Education Outreach Director - Jeremey Whitley

iate Editors - Chad Cicconi & Colleen Boyd

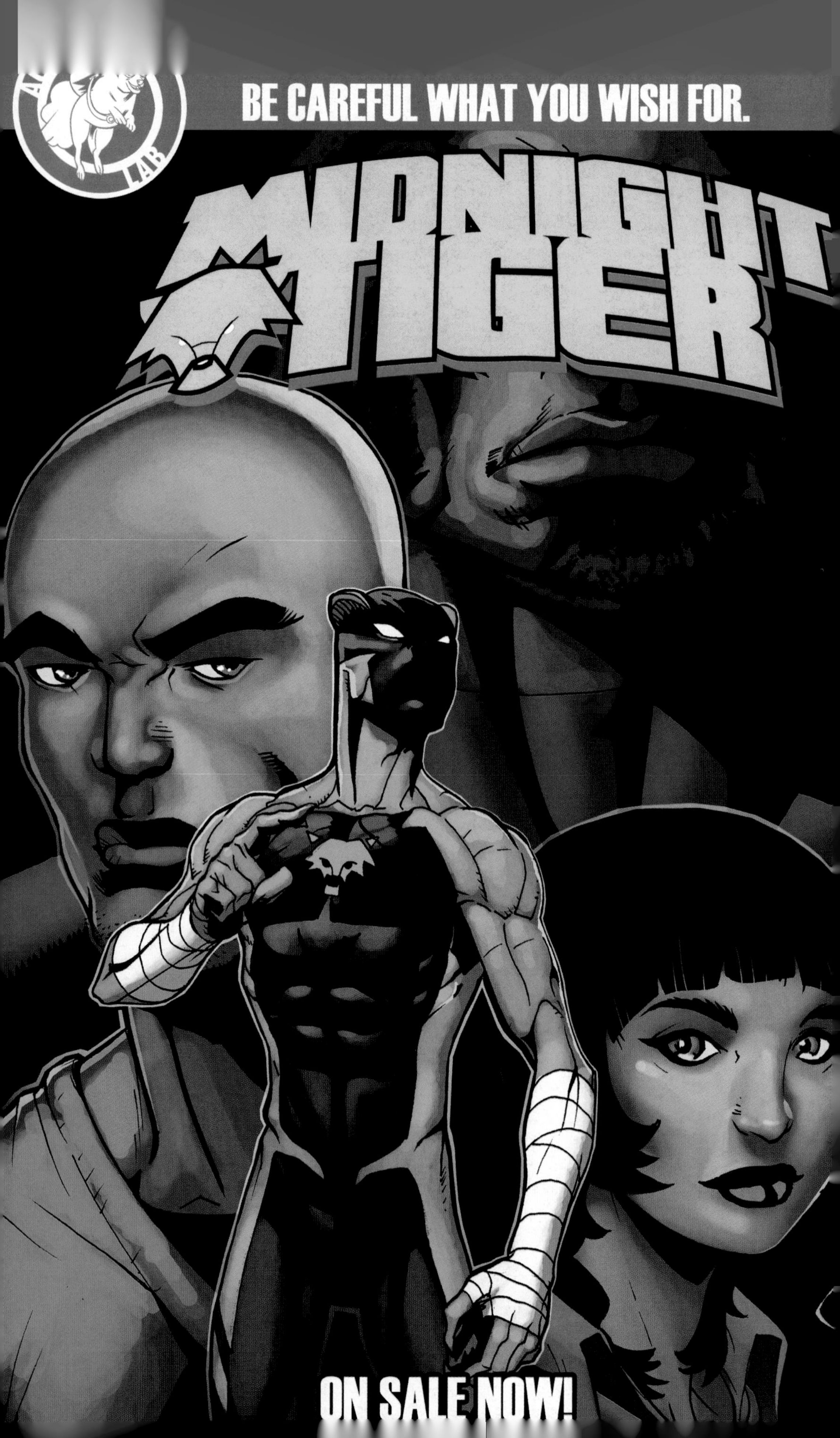
BE CAREFUL WHAT YOU WISH FOR.
MIDNIGHT TIGER
ON SALE NOW!

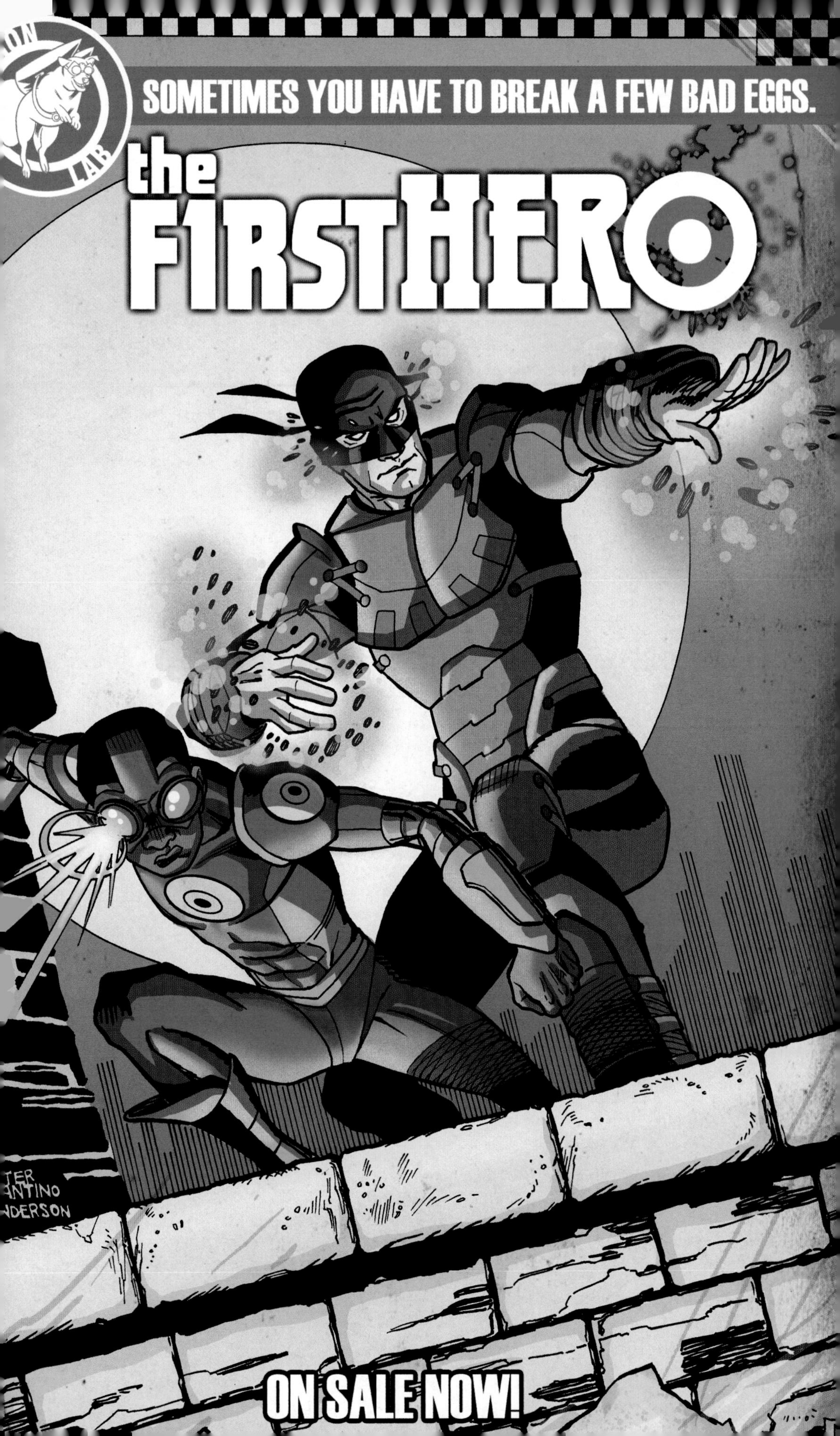
SOMETIMES YOU HAVE TO BREAK A FEW BAD EGGS.
the FIRSTHERO
ON SALE NOW!

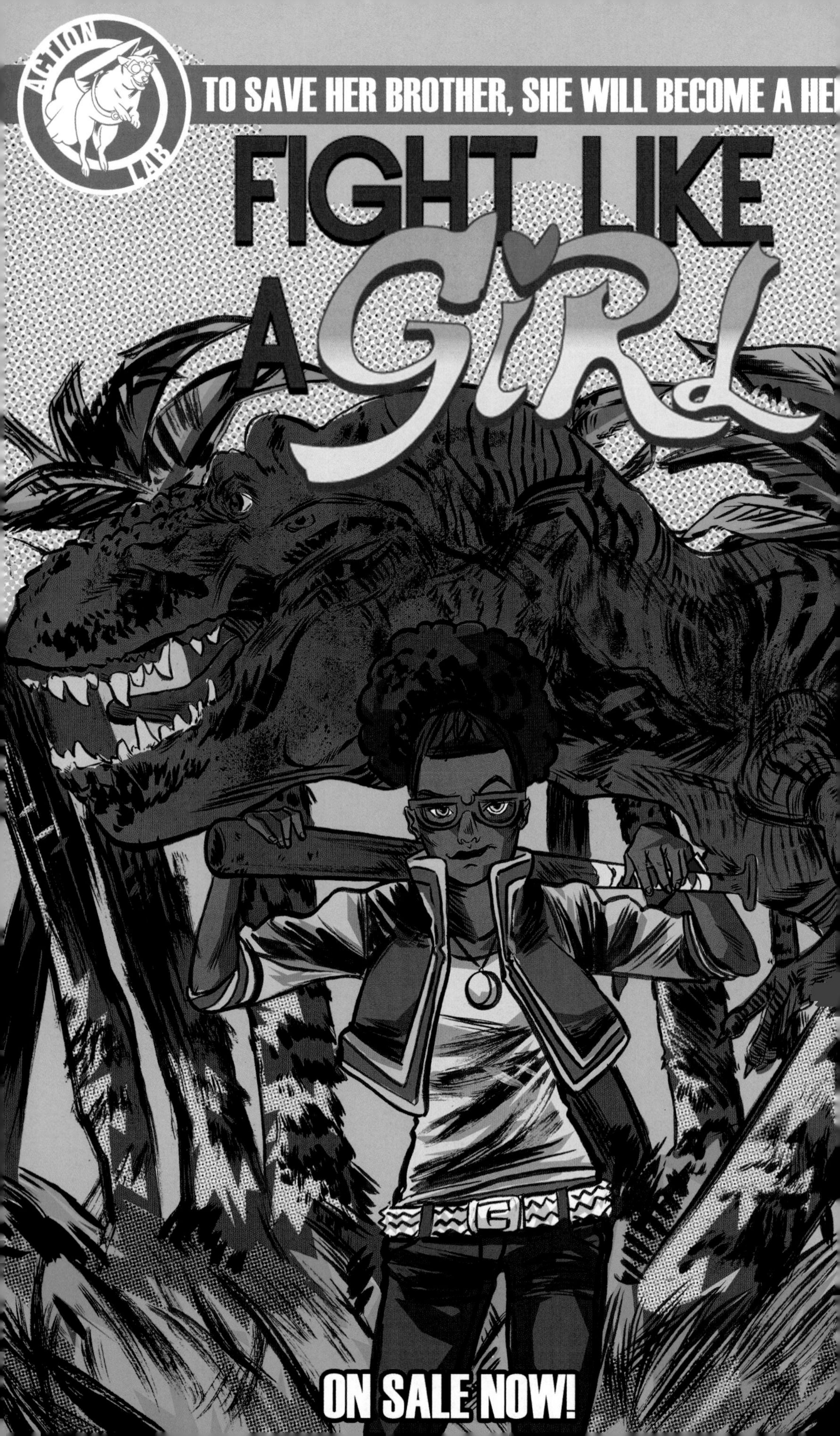

ACTION LAB
TO SAVE HER BROTHER, SHE WILL BECOME A HE
FIGHT LIKE A GIRL
ON SALE NOW!

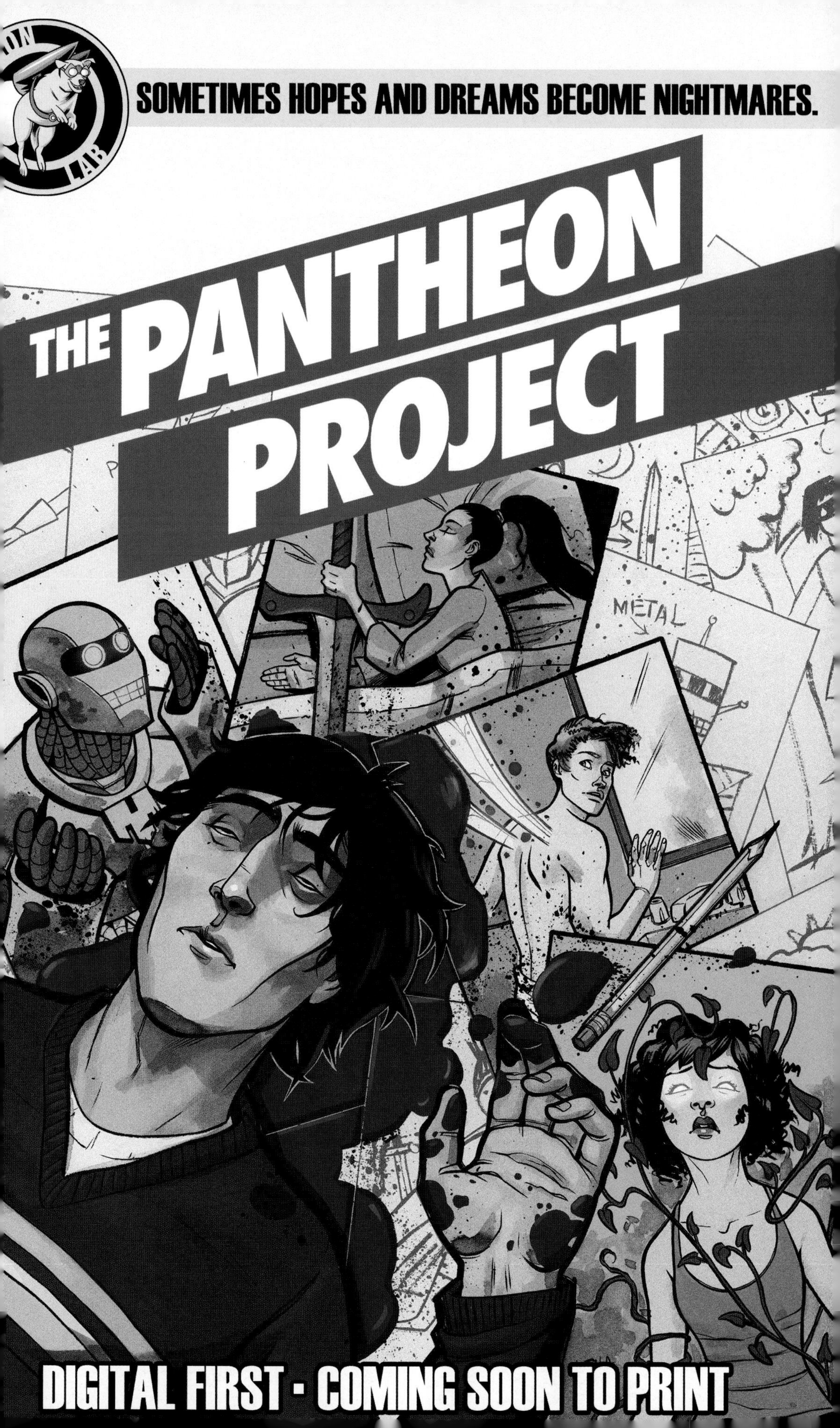
SOMETIMES HOPES AND DREAMS BECOME NIGHTMARES.
THE PANTHEON PROJECT
MÉTAL
DIGITAL FIRST - COMING SOON TO PRINT

MINECRAFT

The official handbooks packed with guides, exclusive interviews and tips from experts!

COMMUNITY CREATIONS
THE MOST IMPRESSIVE ROYAL HALLS IN THE KINGDOM!

DWARVEN CITY
BY FYREUK

This hall was made for the fantasy race of the dwarves. The whole build is situated inside a mountain and in places extends down toward the bedrock layer. There's no natural light at all.

Huge cauldrons of lava light up the room, as does the running lava under the glass and at the back of the hall. Since dwarves are natural miners, it was appropriate to use an excess of gold and iron.

Fror
Const
Han

TIPS TO TAKE FROM THIS BUILD:
Lava can provide a warm light source underground and create a sense of atmosphere.

WARNING: If you're attempting something similar to this, add the lava last. It's very easy to accidentally set yourself or any flammable blocks on fire. Always keep a water bucket in your hotbar to deal with any emergencies.

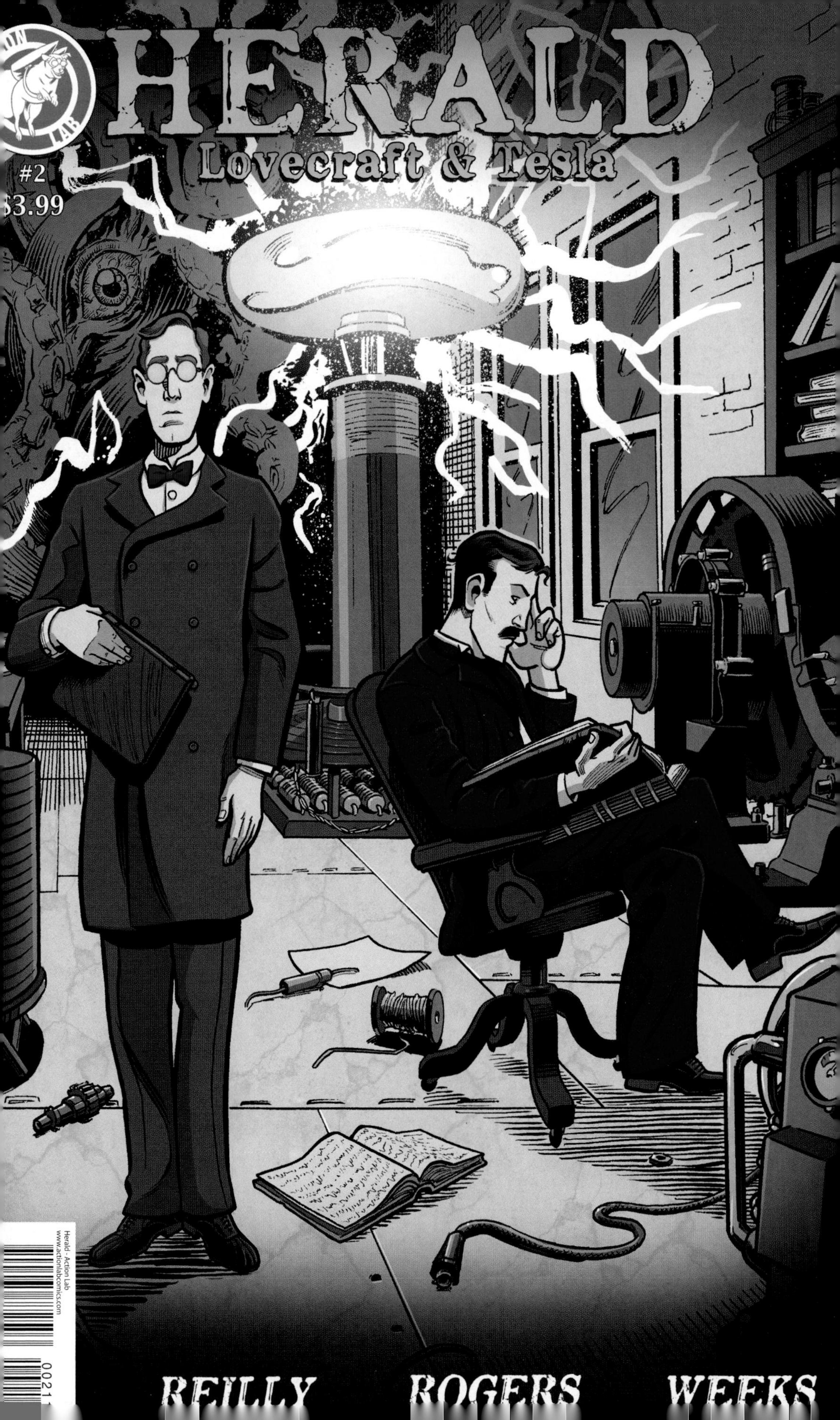
HERALD
Lovecraft & Tesla
#2
$3.99
Herald - Action Lab
www.actionlabcomics.com
REILLY
ROGERS
WEEKS

ꓭERALD
Lovecraft & Tesla

History in the Making
Issue 2 of 3

Written by **John Reilly**

Pencils by **Tom Rogers**

Ink, Color, Letters by **Dexter Weeks**

Logo Design by **Michelle Nikolajevic**

Action Lab Comics

Publisher - **Bryan Seaton**   President - **Kevin Freeman**   Creative Director - **Dave Dwonch**

Editor-in-Chief - **Shawn Gabborin**   Co-Directors of Marketing - **Jamal Igle & Kelly Dale**

Social Media Director - **Jim Dietz**   Education Outreach Director - **Jeremey Whitley**

Associate Editors - **Chad Cicconi & Colleen Boyd**

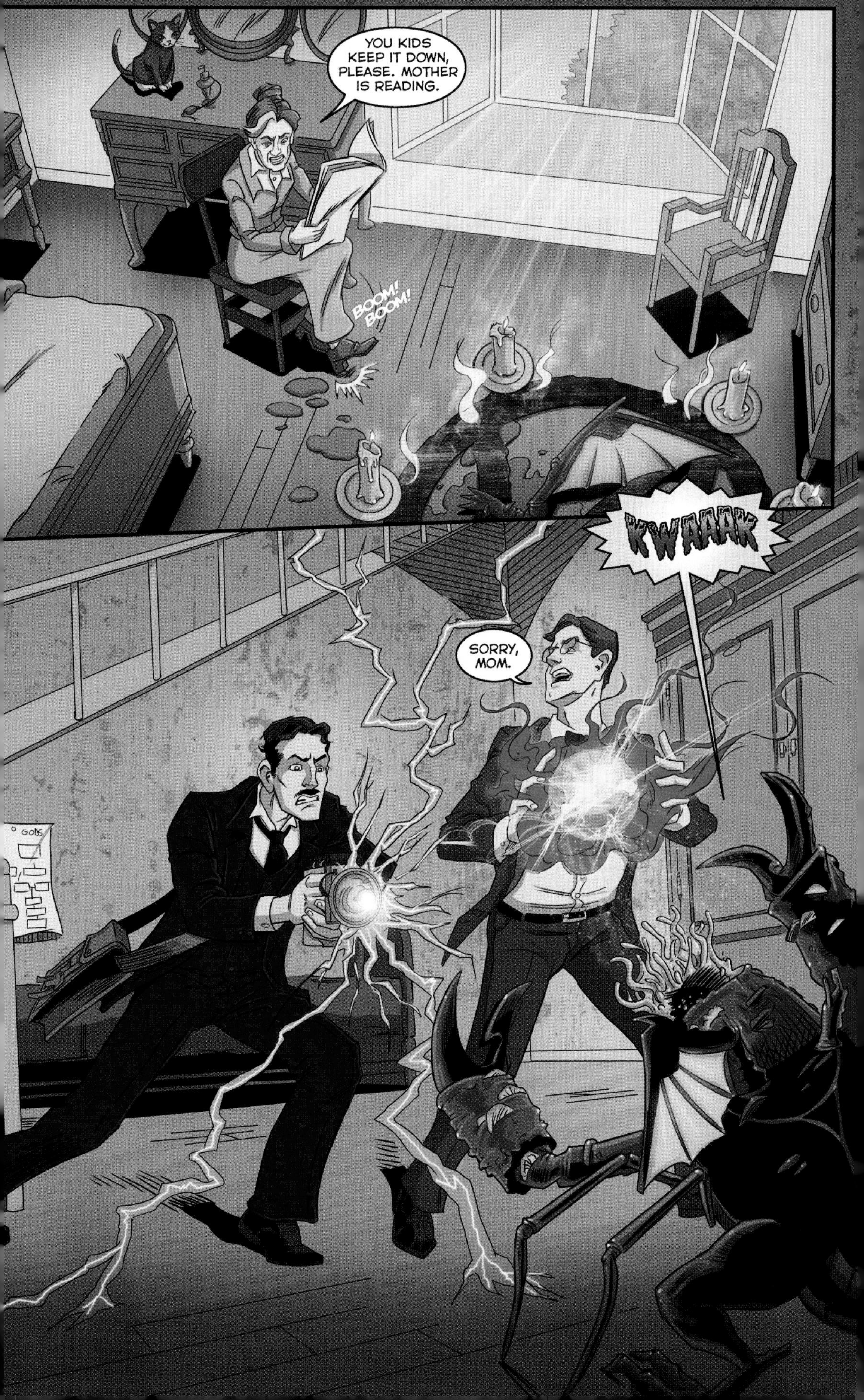
YOU KIDS KEEP IT DOWN, PLEASE. MOTHER IS READING.
BOOM! BOOM!
KWAAAK
SORRY, MOM.
GODS

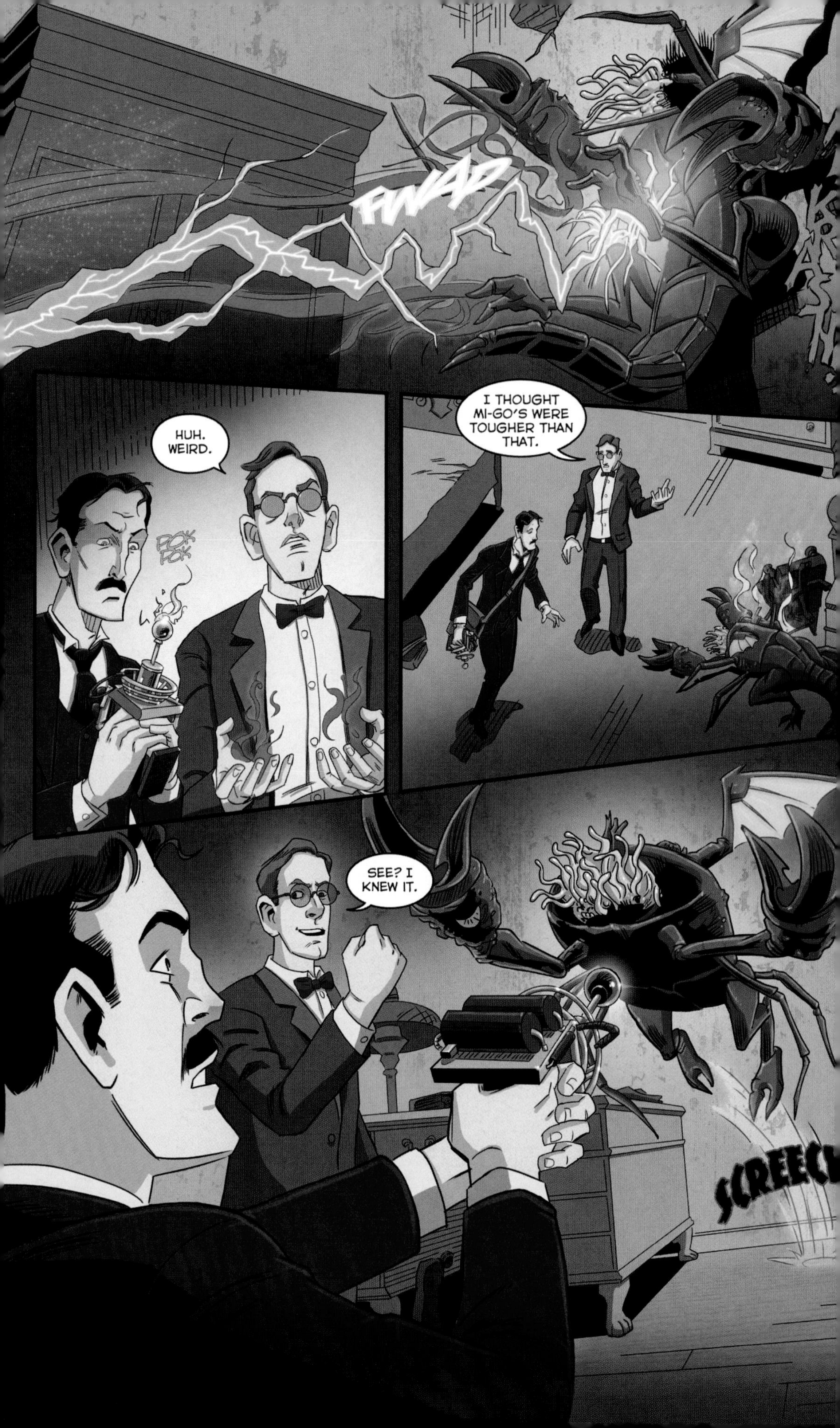
FWAD
HUH. WEIRD.
POK POK
I THOUGHT MI-GO'S WERE TOUGHER THAN THAT.
SEE? I KNEW IT.

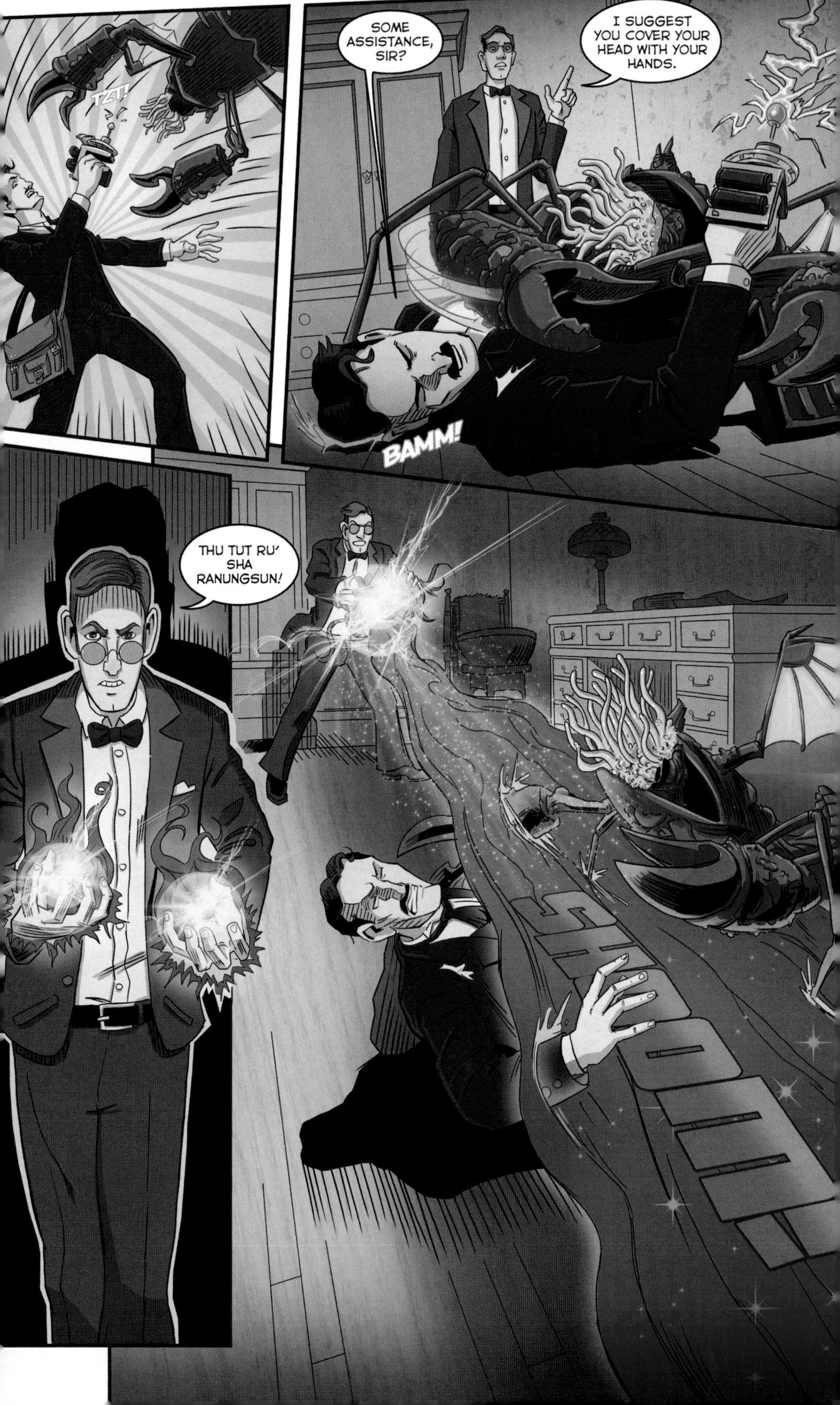
TZT!
SOME ASSISTANCE, SIR?
I SUGGEST YOU COVER YOUR HEAD WITH YOUR HANDS.
BAMM!
THU TUT RU' SHA RANUNGSUN!

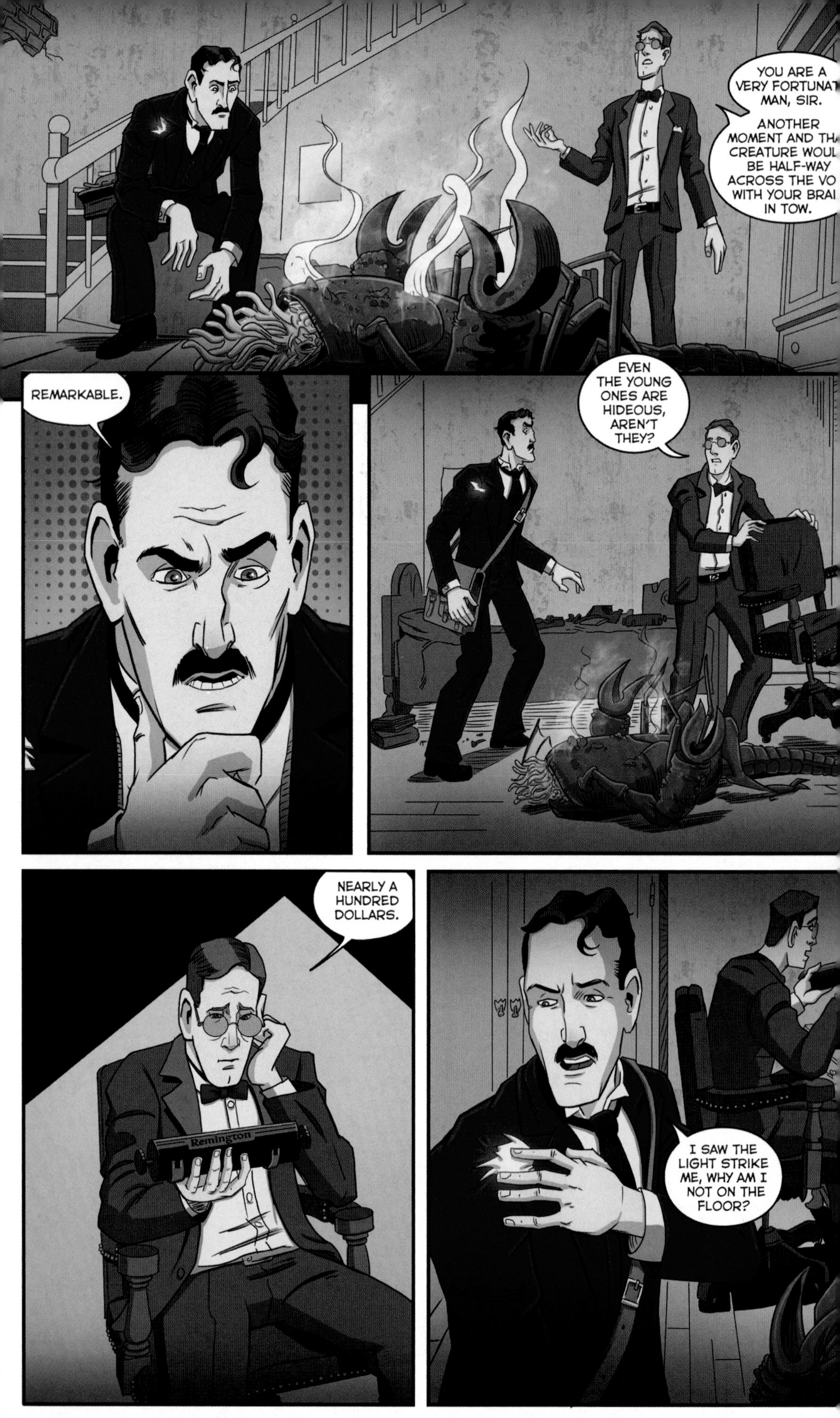
YOU ARE A VERY FORTUNAT MAN, SIR.
ANOTHER MOMENT AND TH CREATURE WOUL BE HALF-WAY ACROSS THE VO WITH YOUR BRAI IN TOW.
REMARKABLE.
EVEN THE YOUNG ONES ARE HIDEOUS, AREN'T THEY?
NEARLY A HUNDRED DOLLARS.
Remington
I SAW THE LIGHT STRIKE ME, WHY AM I NOT ON THE FLOOR?

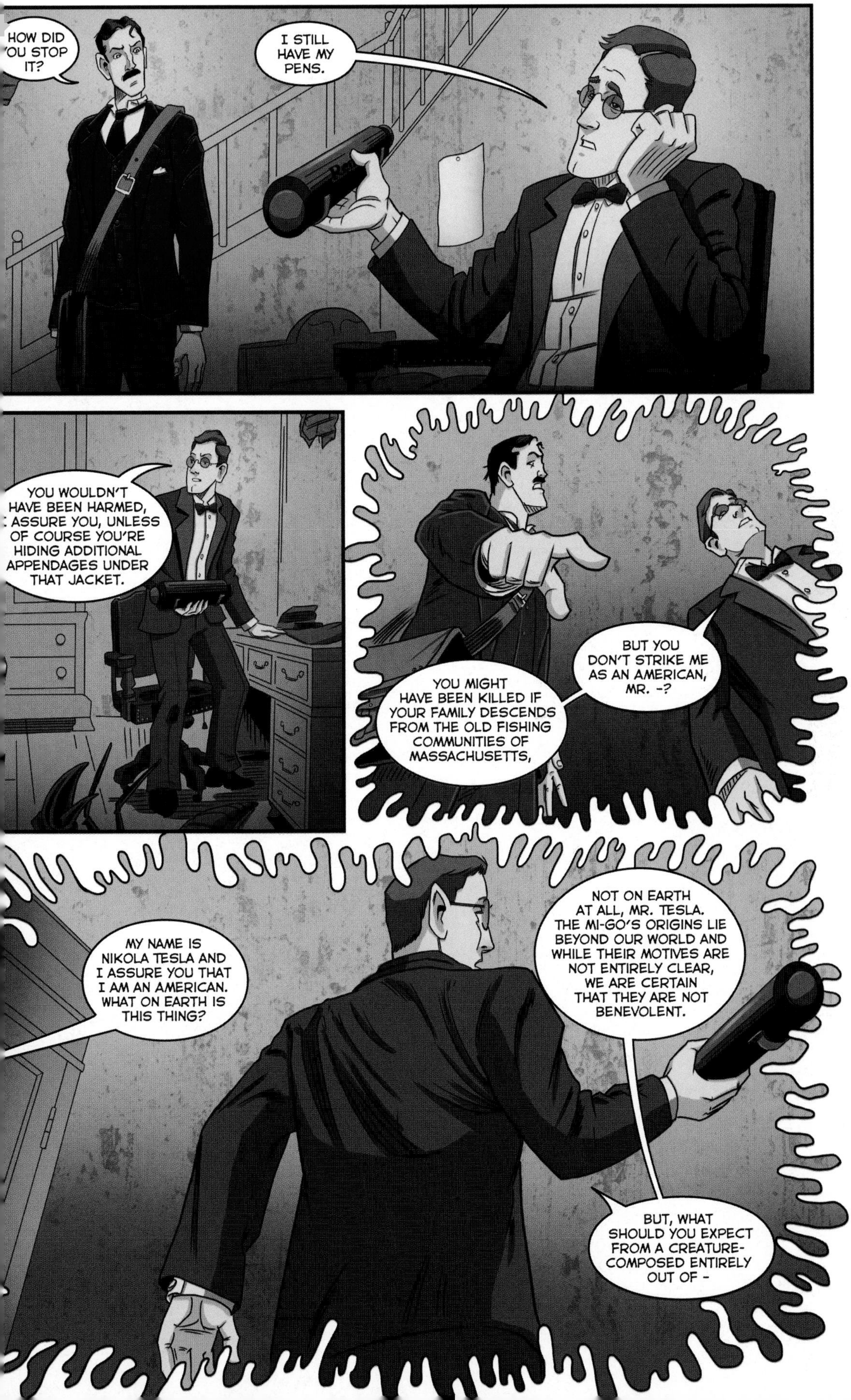
HOW DID YOU STOP IT?
I STILL HAVE MY PENS.
YOU WOULDN'T HAVE BEEN HARMED, I ASSURE YOU, UNLESS OF COURSE YOU'RE HIDING ADDITIONAL APPENDAGES UNDER THAT JACKET.
YOU MIGHT HAVE BEEN KILLED IF YOUR FAMILY DESCENDS FROM THE OLD FISHING COMMUNITIES OF MASSACHUSETTS,
BUT YOU DON'T STRIKE ME AS AN AMERICAN, MR. -?
MY NAME IS NIKOLA TESLA AND I ASSURE YOU THAT I AM AN AMERICAN. WHAT ON EARTH IS THIS THING?
NOT ON EARTH AT ALL, MR. TESLA. THE MI-GO'S ORIGINS LIE BEYOND OUR WORLD AND WHILE THEIR MOTIVES ARE NOT ENTIRELY CLEAR, WE ARE CERTAIN THAT THEY ARE NOT BENEVOLENT.
BUT, WHAT SHOULD YOU EXPECT FROM A CREATURE- COMPOSED ENTIRELY OUT OF -

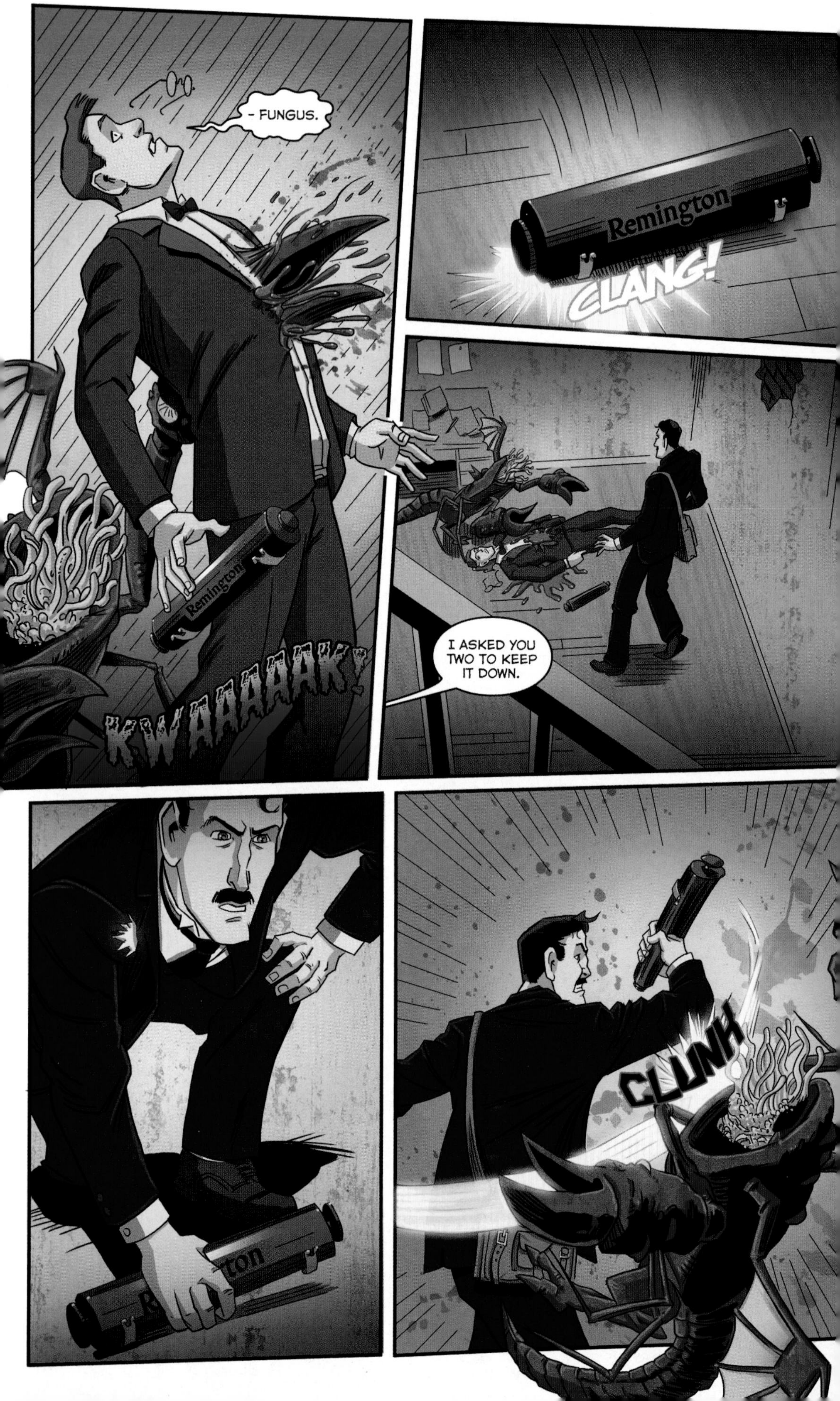

- FUNGUS.
KWAAAAAK!
Remington
CLANG!
I ASKED YOU TWO TO KEEP IT DOWN.
CLUNK

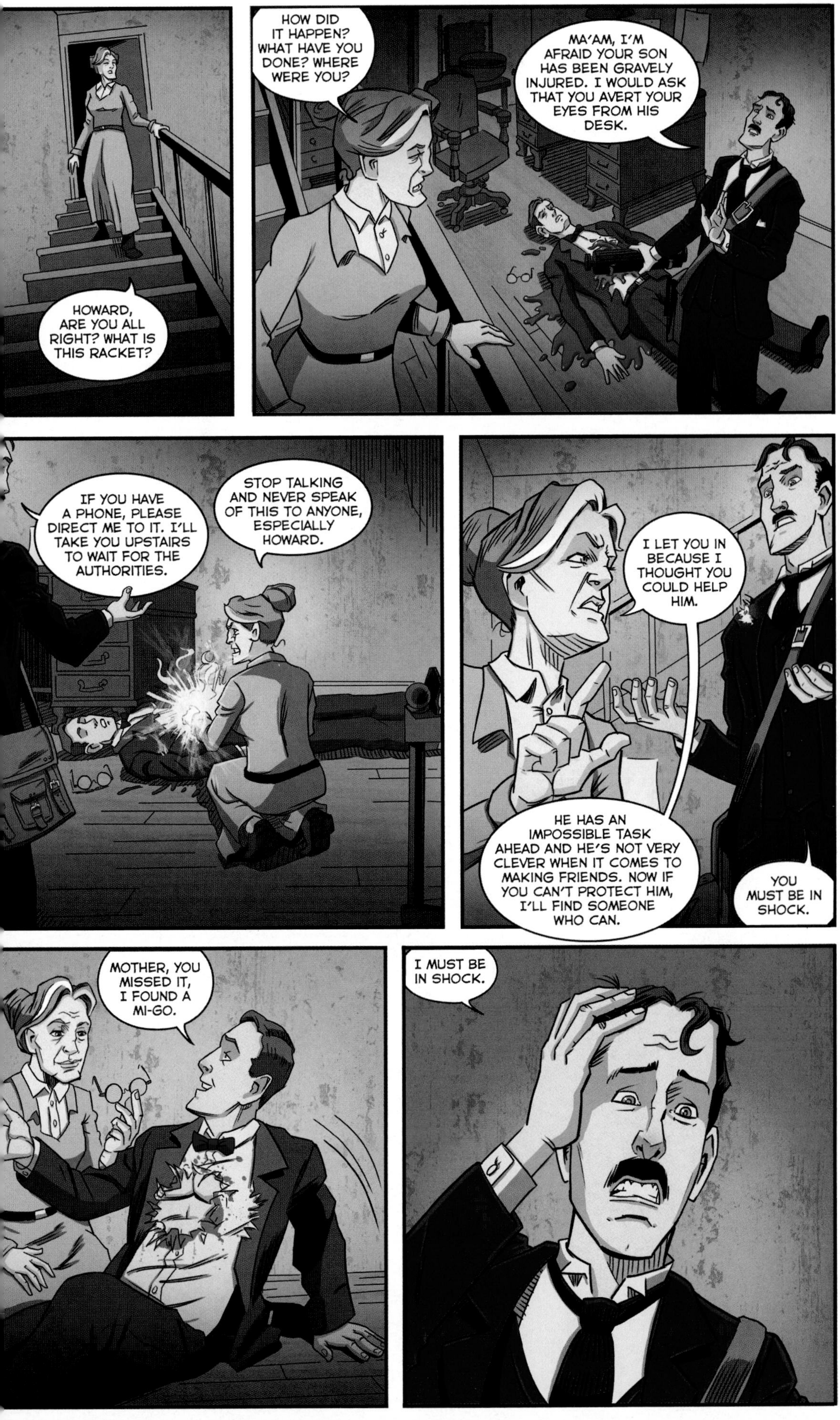
HOWARD, ARE YOU ALL RIGHT? WHAT IS THIS RACKET?
HOW DID IT HAPPEN? WHAT HAVE YOU DONE? WHERE WERE YOU?
MA'AM, I'M AFRAID YOUR SON HAS BEEN GRAVELY INJURED. I WOULD ASK THAT YOU AVERT YOUR EYES FROM HIS DESK.
IF YOU HAVE A PHONE, PLEASE DIRECT ME TO IT. I'LL TAKE YOU UPSTAIRS TO WAIT FOR THE AUTHORITIES.
STOP TALKING AND NEVER SPEAK OF THIS TO ANYONE, ESPECIALLY HOWARD.
I LET YOU IN BECAUSE I THOUGHT YOU COULD HELP HIM.
HE HAS AN IMPOSSIBLE TASK AHEAD AND HE'S NOT VERY CLEVER WHEN IT COMES TO MAKING FRIENDS. NOW IF YOU CAN'T PROTECT HIM, I'LL FIND SOMEONE WHO CAN.
YOU MUST BE IN SHOCK.
MOTHER, YOU MISSED IT, I FOUND A MI-GO.
I MUST BE IN SHOCK.

YOU WON'T FIND IT IN THERE.

IF WE HAD A COPY OF THE NECRONOMICON, WE CERTAINLY WOULDN'T KEEP IT IN THE HOUSE.

YOU'RE GOING TO RUIN YOUR TROUSERS IF YOU SIT ON THE FLOOR LIKE THAT.

I REMEMBER READING SOMETHING ABOUT IT.

NOT A COPY, BUT A – YES, HERE. LOOK, MY PROFESSOR AT BROWN HAD US STUDY PORTIONS OF IT. HE'LL KNOW WHERE TO FIND ONE.

FOR A BOOK WRITTEN IN THE MIDDLE AGES THAT SUPPOSEDLY EXPOUNDS ON DIMENSIONAL TRAVEL?

NOT EXACTLY AS SUCH, BUT THE NECRONOMICON WOULD BE THE SMARTEST PLACE TO LOOK, GIVEN YOUR PREDICAMENT.

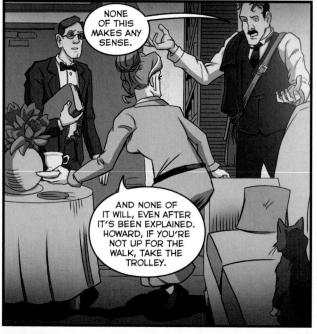

NONE OF THIS MAKES ANY SENSE.

AND NONE OF IT WILL, EVEN AFTER IT'S BEEN EXPLAINED. HOWARD, IF YOU'RE NOT UP FOR THE WALK, TAKE THE TROLLEY.

MR. TESLA, LET ME SEE YOUR JACKET, IF YOU WOULD.

I *WAS* GOING TO CHANGE, MOTHER.

HOWARD, DEAR, GO CHANGE. YOU WON'T BE SEEN IN PUBLIC WEARING A SHIRT LIKE THAT.

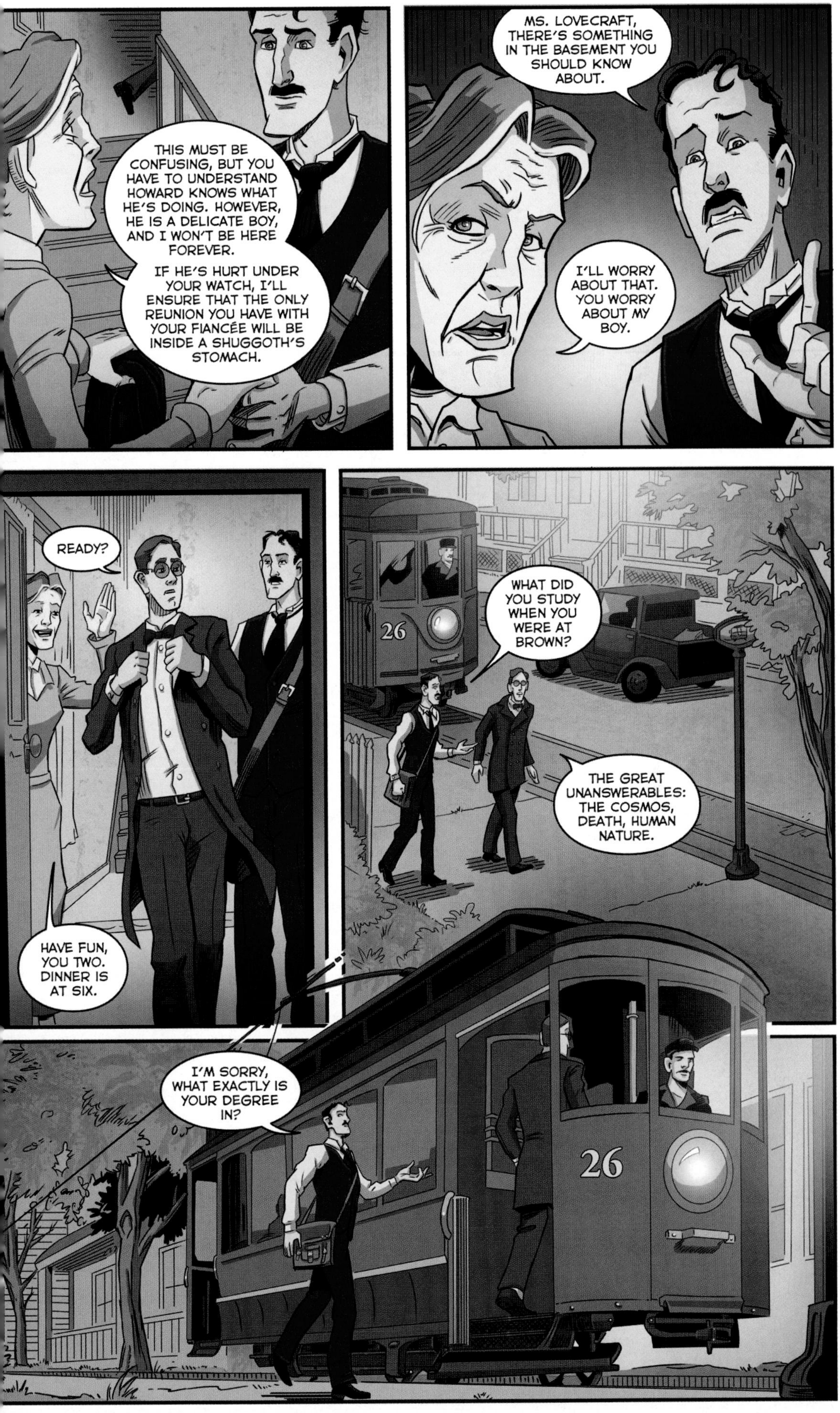
THIS MUST BE CONFUSING, BUT YOU HAVE TO UNDERSTAND HOWARD KNOWS WHAT HE'S DOING. HOWEVER, HE IS A DELICATE BOY, AND I WON'T BE HERE FOREVER.
IF HE'S HURT UNDER YOUR WATCH, I'LL ENSURE THAT THE ONLY REUNION YOU HAVE WITH YOUR FIANCÉE WILL BE INSIDE A SHUGGOTH'S STOMACH.
MS. LOVECRAFT, THERE'S SOMETHING IN THE BASEMENT YOU SHOULD KNOW ABOUT.
I'LL WORRY ABOUT THAT. YOU WORRY ABOUT MY BOY.
READY?
HAVE FUN, YOU TWO. DINNER IS AT SIX.
26
WHAT DID YOU STUDY WHEN YOU WERE AT BROWN?
THE GREAT UNANSWERABLES: THE COSMOS, DEATH, HUMAN NATURE.
I'M SORRY, WHAT EXACTLY IS YOUR DEGREE IN?
26

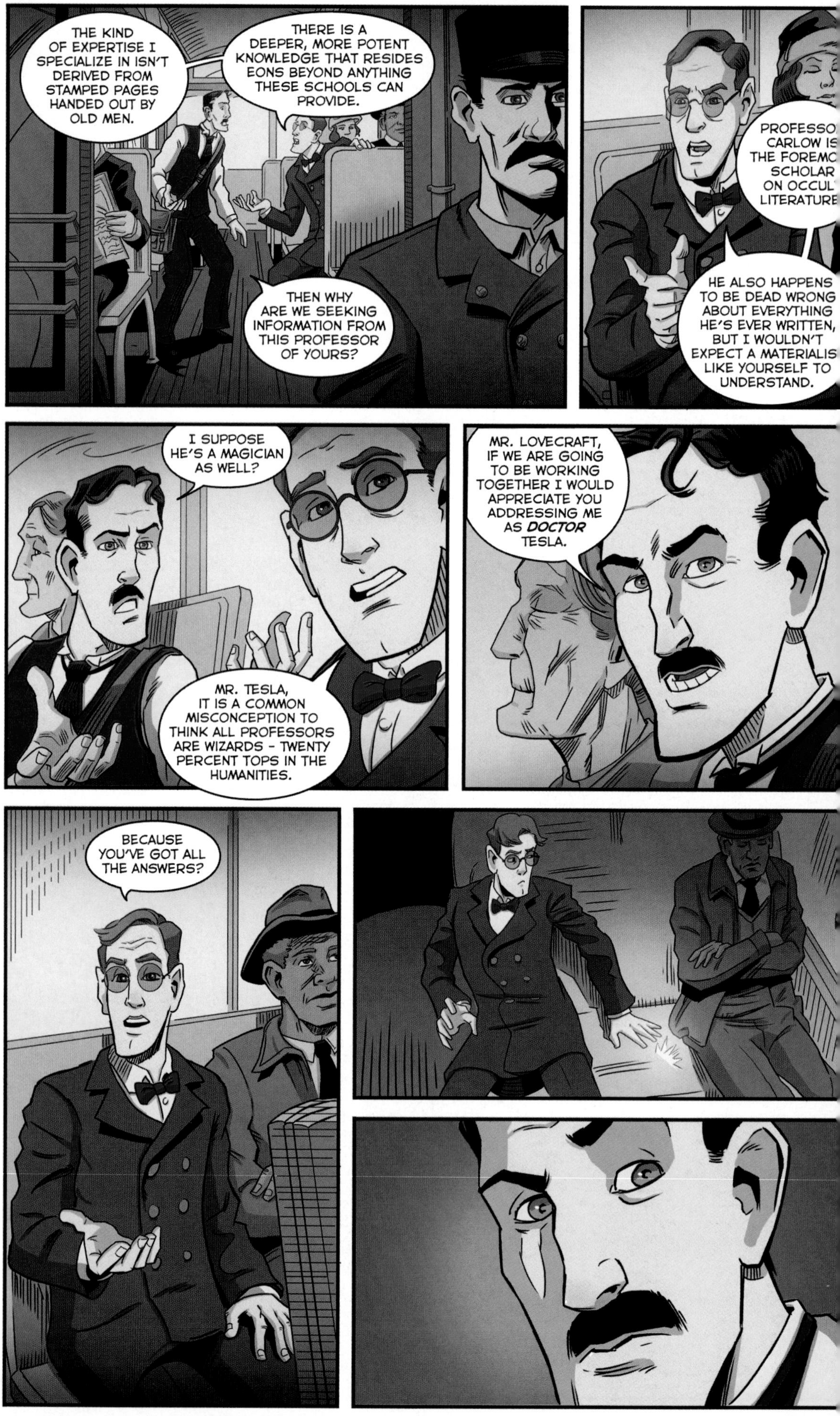
THE KIND OF EXPERTISE I SPECIALIZE IN ISN'T DERIVED FROM STAMPED PAGES HANDED OUT BY OLD MEN.
THERE IS A DEEPER, MORE POTENT KNOWLEDGE THAT RESIDES EONS BEYOND ANYTHING THESE SCHOOLS CAN PROVIDE.
THEN WHY ARE WE SEEKING INFORMATION FROM THIS PROFESSOR OF YOURS?
PROFESSO CARLOW IS THE FOREMO SCHOLAR ON OCCUL LITERATURE
HE ALSO HAPPENS TO BE DEAD WRONG ABOUT EVERYTHING HE'S EVER WRITTEN, BUT I WOULDN'T EXPECT A MATERIALIS LIKE YOURSELF TO UNDERSTAND.
I SUPPOSE HE'S A MAGICIAN AS WELL?
MR. TESLA, IT IS A COMMON MISCONCEPTION TO THINK ALL PROFESSORS ARE WIZARDS - TWENTY PERCENT TOPS IN THE HUMANITIES.
MR. LOVECRAFT, IF WE ARE GOING TO BE WORKING TOGETHER I WOULD APPRECIATE YOU ADDRESSING ME AS ***DOCTOR*** TESLA.
BECAUSE YOU'VE GOT ALL THE ANSWERS?

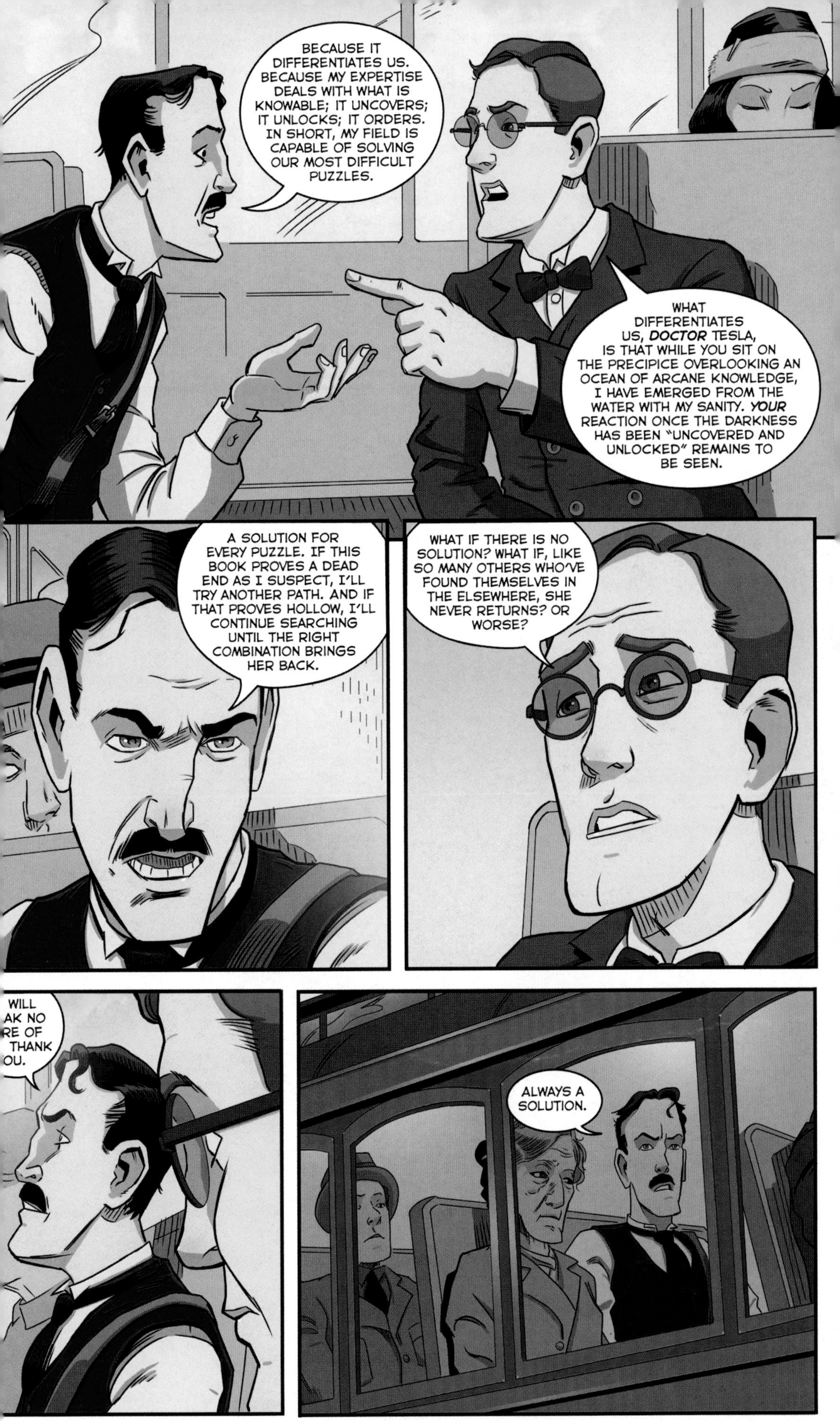
BECAUSE IT DIFFERENTIATES US. BECAUSE MY EXPERTISE DEALS WITH WHAT IS KNOWABLE; IT UNCOVERS; IT UNLOCKS; IT ORDERS. IN SHORT, MY FIELD IS CAPABLE OF SOLVING OUR MOST DIFFICULT PUZZLES.
WHAT DIFFERENTIATES US, DOCTOR TESLA, IS THAT WHILE YOU SIT ON THE PRECIPICE OVERLOOKING AN OCEAN OF ARCANE KNOWLEDGE, I HAVE EMERGED FROM THE WATER WITH MY SANITY. YOUR REACTION ONCE THE DARKNESS HAS BEEN "UNCOVERED AND UNLOCKED" REMAINS TO BE SEEN.
A SOLUTION FOR EVERY PUZZLE. IF THIS BOOK PROVES A DEAD END AS I SUSPECT, I'LL TRY ANOTHER PATH. AND IF THAT PROVES HOLLOW, I'LL CONTINUE SEARCHING UNTIL THE RIGHT COMBINATION BRINGS HER BACK.
WHAT IF THERE IS NO SOLUTION? WHAT IF, LIKE SO MANY OTHERS WHO'VE FOUND THEMSELVES IN THE ELSEWHERE, SHE NEVER RETURNS? OR WORSE?
WILL AK NO RE OF THANK OU.
ALWAYS A SOLUTION.

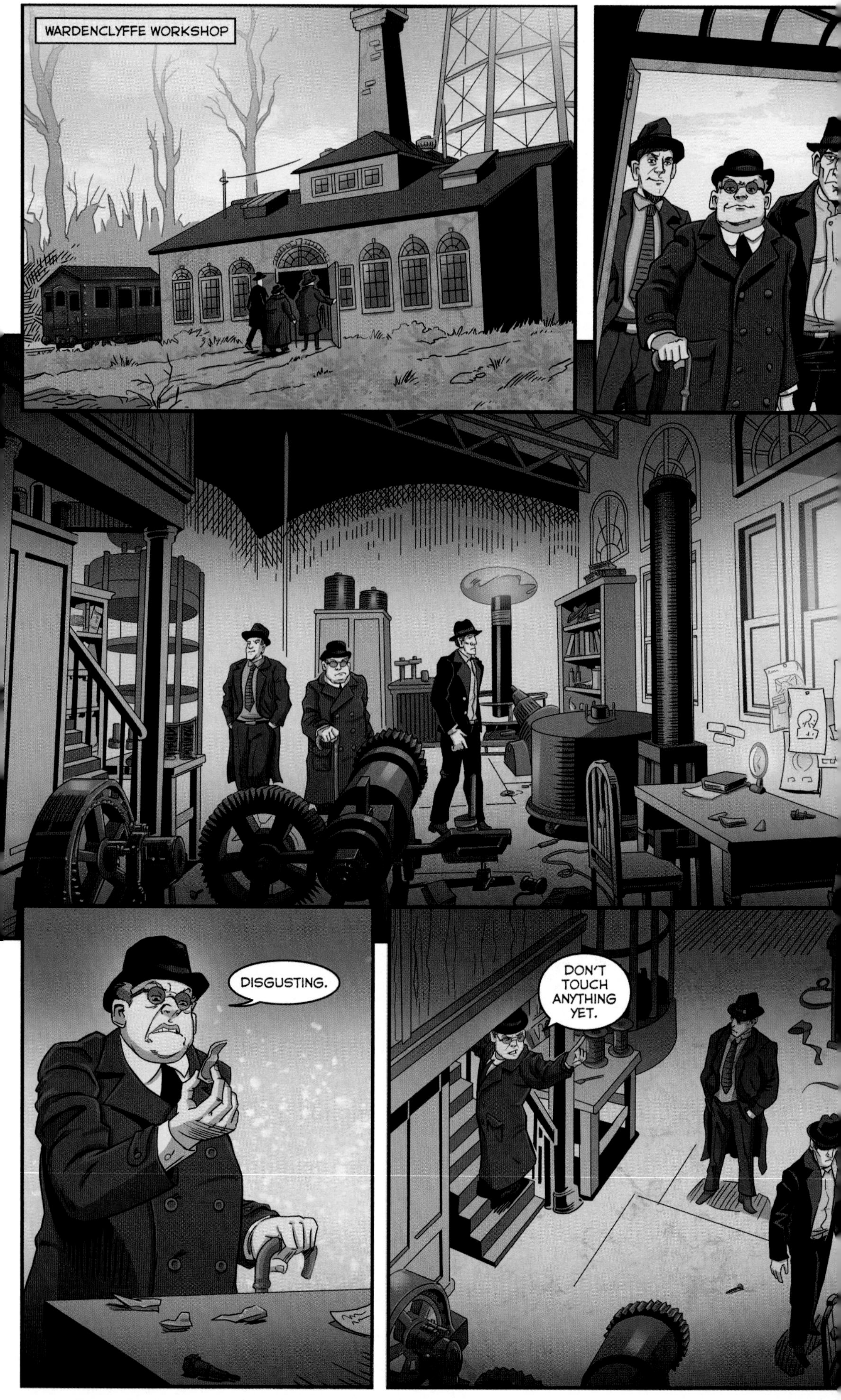
WARDENCLYFFE WORKSHOP
DISGUSTING.
DON'T TOUCH ANYTHING YET.

WHAT MYSTERIES HAVE YOU LEFT US?

ZZZZERB

QUIT GOOFING AROUND, WE NEED TO INVENTORY EVERYTHING BEFORE WE TAKE IT.

YOU WANT HIS MAIL?

EDISON'S MAIL. ALL OF THIS IS HIS NOW.

BEGIN LOADING WHATEVER YOU THINK WON'T KILL YOU.

Albert Einstein   Nikola Tesla
Wardenclyffe Tower
NY 11101

STOP. TAKE THIS FIRST.

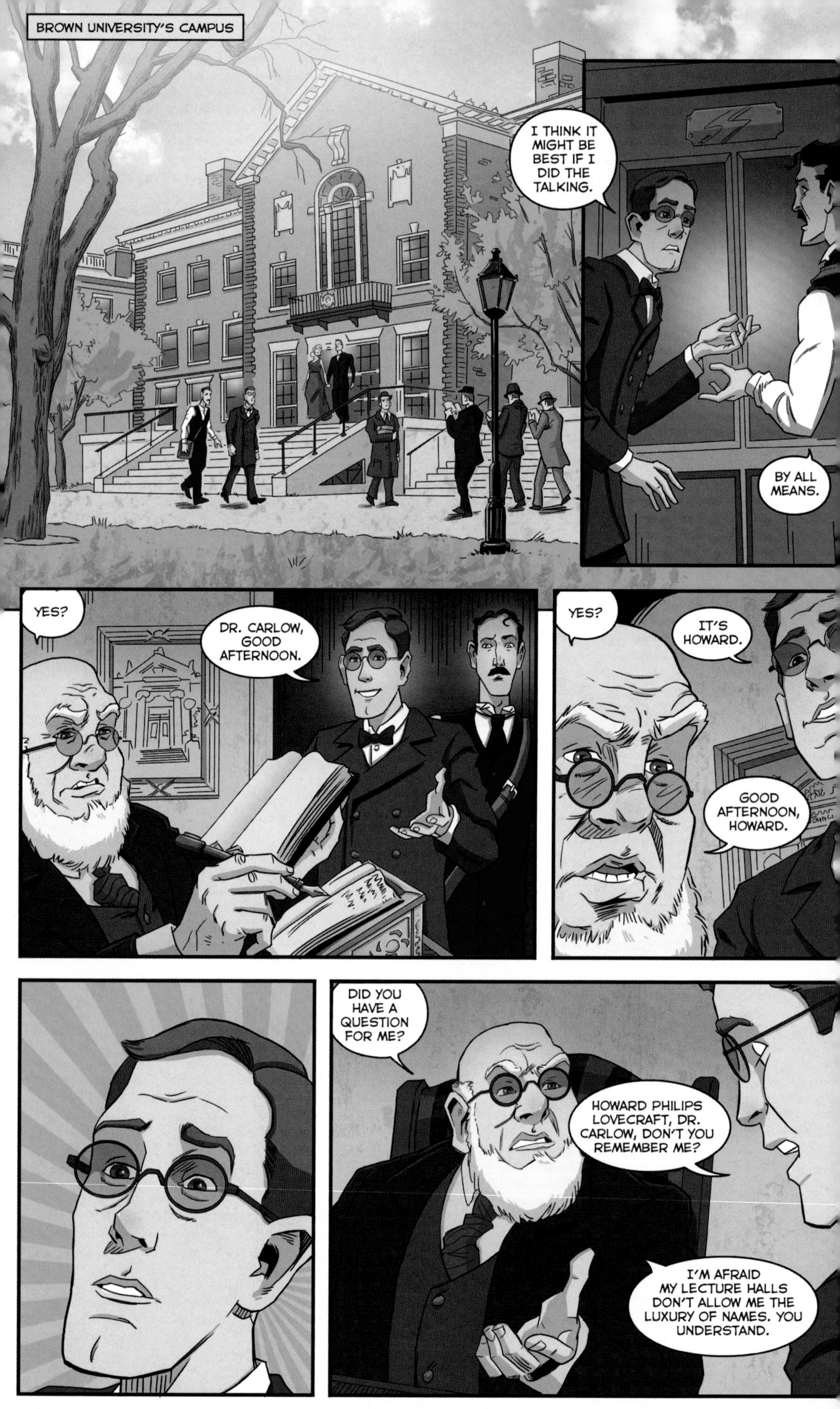
BROWN UNIVERSITY'S CAMPUS
I THINK IT MIGHT BE BEST IF I DID THE TALKING.
BY ALL MEANS.
YES?
DR. CARLOW, GOOD AFTERNOON.
YES?
IT'S HOWARD.
GOOD AFTERNOON, HOWARD.
DID YOU HAVE A QUESTION FOR ME?
HOWARD PHILIPS LOVECRAFT, DR. CARLOW, DON'T YOU REMEMBER ME?
I'M AFRAID MY LECTURE HALLS DON'T ALLOW ME THE LUXURY OF NAMES. YOU UNDERSTAND.

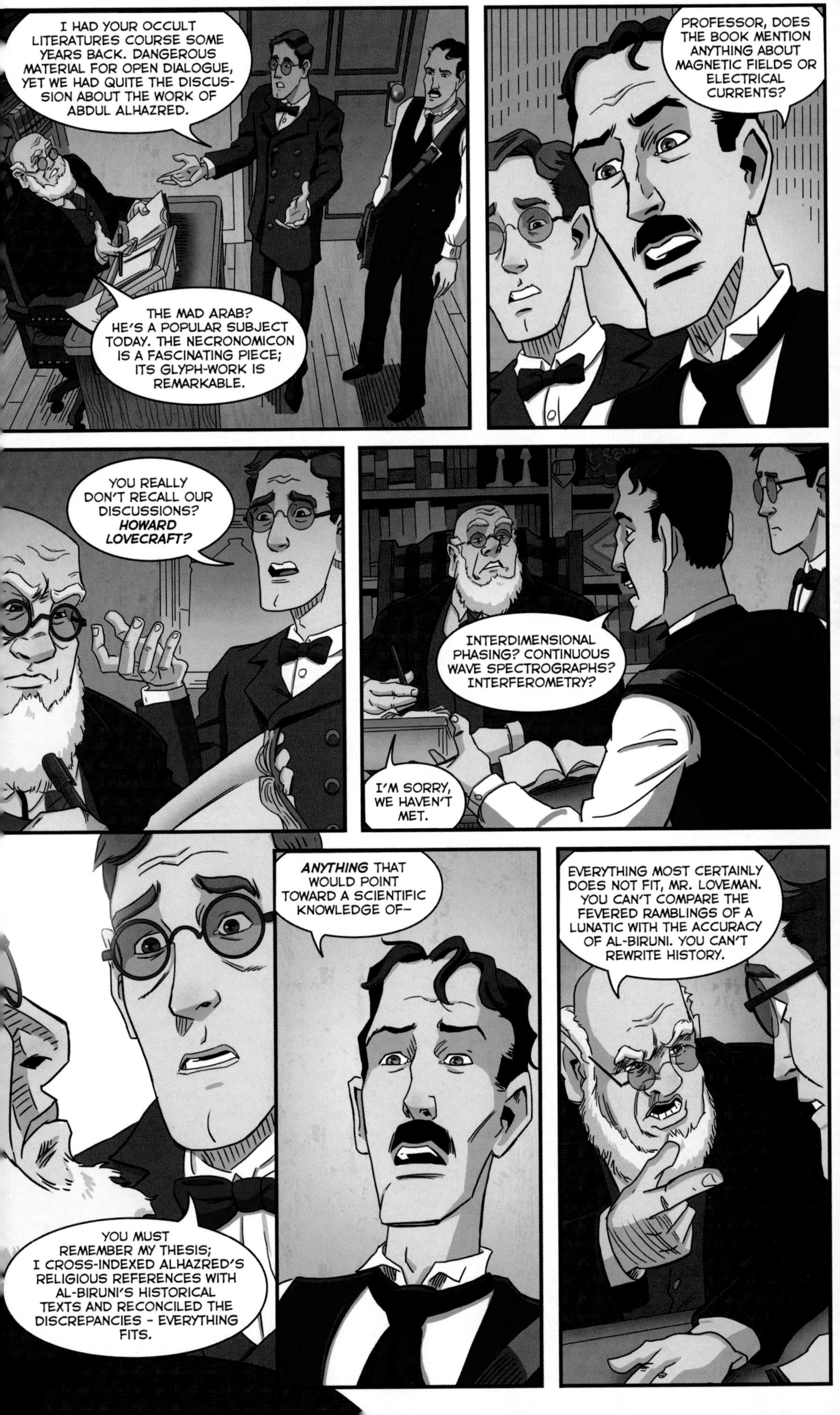

I HAD YOUR OCCULT LITERATURES COURSE SOME YEARS BACK. DANGEROUS MATERIAL FOR OPEN DIALOGUE, YET WE HAD QUITE THE DISCUSSION ABOUT THE WORK OF ABDUL ALHAZRED.
THE MAD ARAB? HE'S A POPULAR SUBJECT TODAY. THE NECRONOMICON IS A FASCINATING PIECE; ITS GLYPH-WORK IS REMARKABLE.
PROFESSOR, DOES THE BOOK MENTION ANYTHING ABOUT MAGNETIC FIELDS OR ELECTRICAL CURRENTS?
YOU REALLY DON'T RECALL OUR DISCUSSIONS? *HOWARD LOVECRAFT?*
INTERDIMENSIONAL PHASING? CONTINUOUS WAVE SPECTROGRAPHS? INTERFEROMETRY?
I'M SORRY, WE HAVEN'T MET.
YOU MUST REMEMBER MY THESIS; I CROSS-INDEXED ALHAZRED'S RELIGIOUS REFERENCES WITH AL-BIRUNI'S HISTORICAL TEXTS AND RECONCILED THE DISCREPANCIES - EVERYTHING FITS.
ANYTHING THAT WOULD POINT TOWARD A SCIENTIFIC KNOWLEDGE OF-
EVERYTHING MOST CERTAINLY DOES NOT FIT, MR. LOVEMAN. YOU CAN'T COMPARE THE FEVERED RAMBLINGS OF A LUNATIC WITH THE ACCURACY OF AL-BIRUNI. YOU CAN'T REWRITE HISTORY.

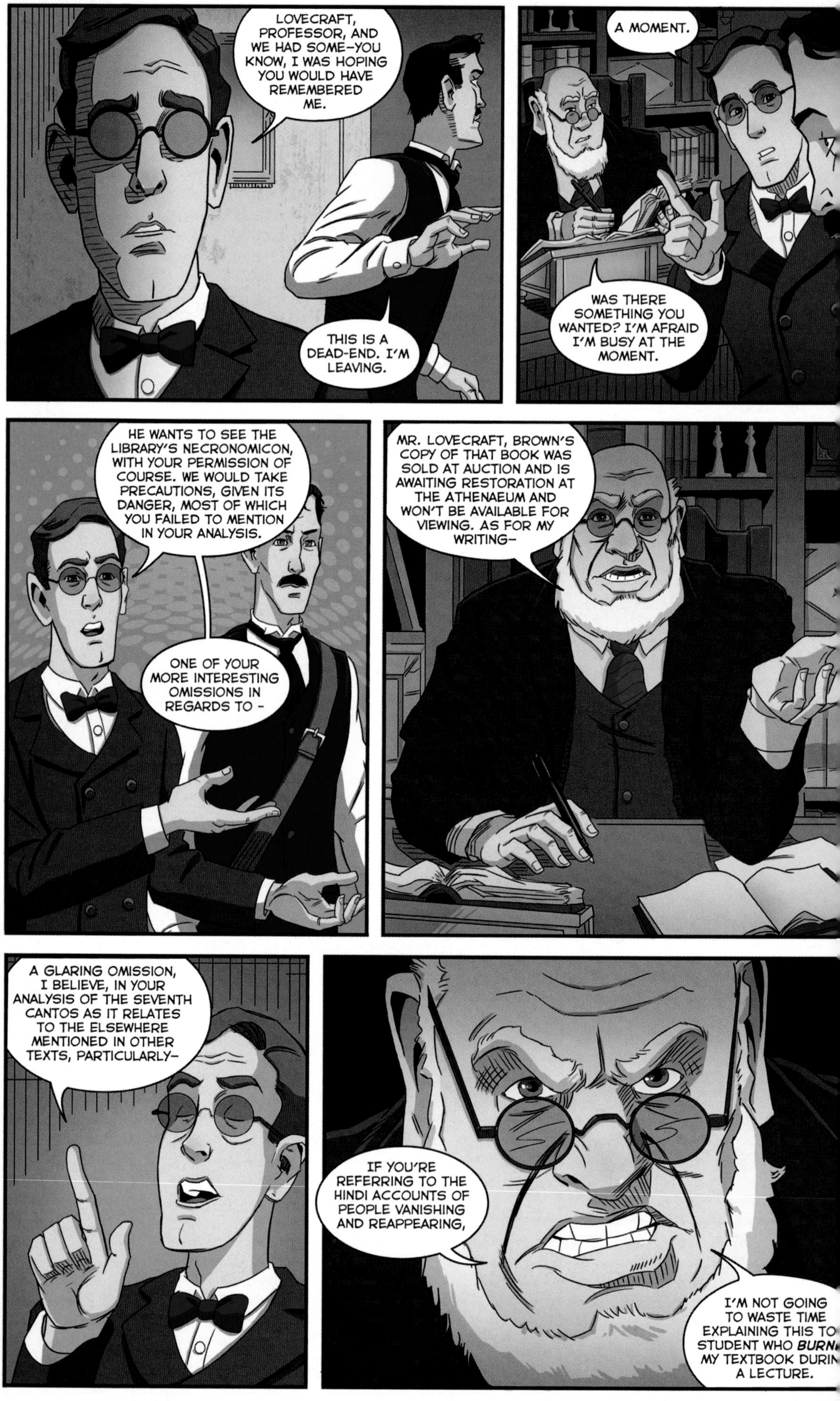

LOVECRAFT, PROFESSOR, AND WE HAD SOME—YOU KNOW, I WAS HOPING YOU WOULD HAVE REMEMBERED ME.
THIS IS A DEAD-END. I'M LEAVING.
A MOMENT.
WAS THERE SOMETHING YOU WANTED? I'M AFRAID I'M BUSY AT THE MOMENT.
HE WANTS TO SEE THE LIBRARY'S NECRONOMICON, WITH YOUR PERMISSION OF COURSE. WE WOULD TAKE PRECAUTIONS, GIVEN ITS DANGER, MOST OF WHICH YOU FAILED TO MENTION IN YOUR ANALYSIS.
ONE OF YOUR MORE INTERESTING OMISSIONS IN REGARDS TO -
MR. LOVECRAFT, BROWN'S COPY OF THAT BOOK WAS SOLD AT AUCTION AND IS AWAITING RESTORATION AT THE ATHENAEUM AND WON'T BE AVAILABLE FOR VIEWING. AS FOR MY WRITING–
A GLARING OMISSION, I BELIEVE, IN YOUR ANALYSIS OF THE SEVENTH CANTOS AS IT RELATES TO THE ELSEWHERE MENTIONED IN OTHER TEXTS, PARTICULARLY–
IF YOU'RE REFERRING TO THE HINDI ACCOUNTS OF PEOPLE VANISHING AND REAPPEARING,
I'M NOT GOING TO WASTE TIME EXPLAINING THIS TO STUDENT WHO *BURN* MY TEXTBOOK DURIN A LECTURE.

OU DO MEMBER ME.

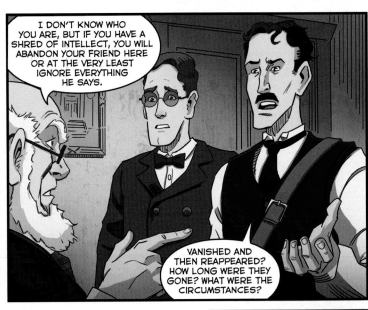

I DON'T KNOW WHO YOU ARE, BUT IF YOU HAVE A SHRED OF INTELLECT, YOU WILL ABANDON YOUR FRIEND HERE OR AT THE VERY LEAST IGNORE EVERYTHING HE SAYS.

VANISHED AND THEN REAPPEARED? HOW LONG WERE THEY GONE? WHAT WERE THE CIRCUMSTANCES?

E BOOK *CHOSE* IGNITE WHEN I UCHED IT, I CAN RDLY BE HELD CCOUNTABLE.

IF YOU'D READ MY TREATISE ON RCANE VISION-PLANES, OU'D KNOW THAT KIND OF THING WAS BOUND TO HAPPEN.

MAGIC DOES NOT EXIST, YOUNG MAN, DESPITE YOUR MOST ARDENT ASSERTIONS.

AND YOUR SCHOLARSHIP, DR. CARLOW, IS USELESS, DESPITE YOUR PUBLICATION RECORD.

WAIT, DOES IT SAY HOW THEY RETURNED OR WHERE THEY WENT? WAS A PROCEDURE OUTLINED? WHICH TEXTS?

OUT!

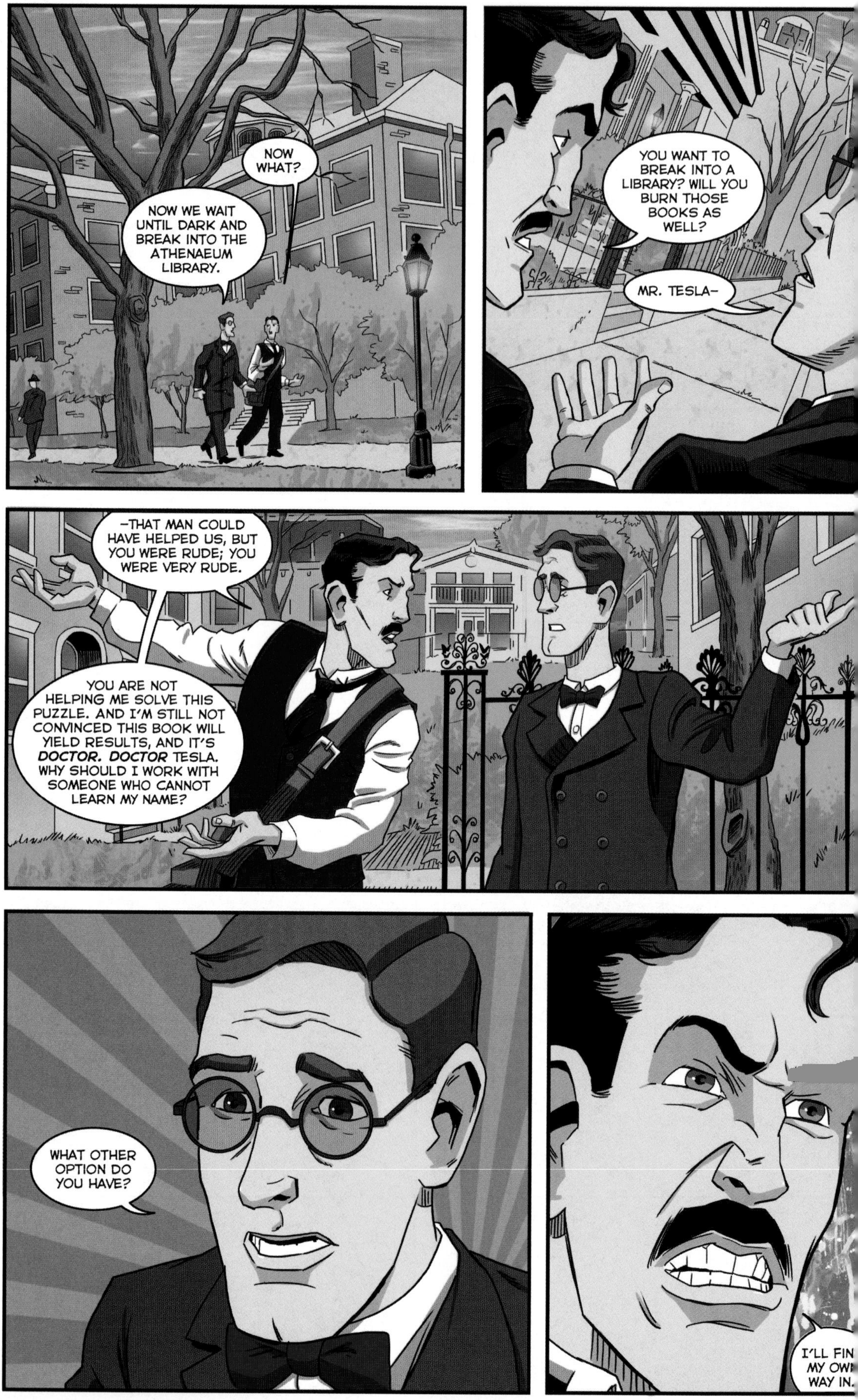
NOW WHAT?
NOW WE WAIT UNTIL DARK AND BREAK INTO THE ATHENAEUM LIBRARY.
YOU WANT TO BREAK INTO A LIBRARY? WILL YOU BURN THOSE BOOKS AS WELL?
MR. TESLA–
–THAT MAN COULD HAVE HELPED US, BUT YOU WERE RUDE; YOU WERE VERY RUDE.
YOU ARE NOT HELPING ME SOLVE THIS PUZZLE. AND I'M STILL NOT CONVINCED THIS BOOK WILL YIELD RESULTS, AND IT'S ***DOCTOR. DOCTOR*** TESLA. WHY SHOULD I WORK WITH SOMEONE WHO CANNOT LEARN MY NAME?
WHAT OTHER OPTION DO YOU HAVE?
I'LL FIN
MY OW
WAY IN.

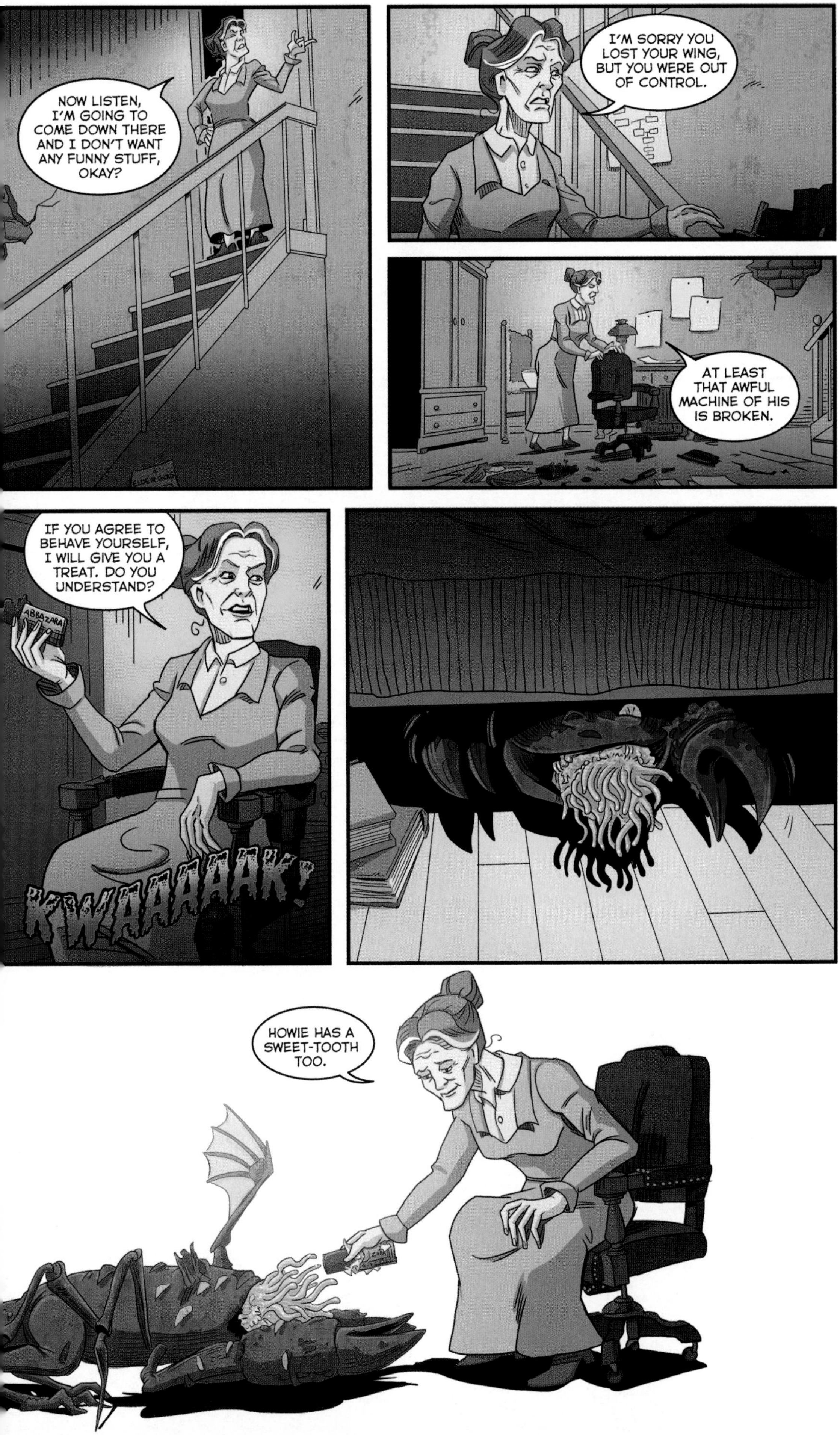
NOW LISTEN, I'M GOING TO COME DOWN THERE AND I DON'T WANT ANY FUNNY STUFF, OKAY?
I'M SORRY YOU LOST YOUR WING, BUT YOU WERE OUT OF CONTROL.
AT LEAST THAT AWFUL MACHINE OF HIS IS BROKEN.
IF YOU AGREE TO BEHAVE YOURSELF, I WILL GIVE YOU A TREAT. DO YOU UNDERSTAND?
ABBAZARA
KWAAAAAK!
HOWIE HAS A SWEET-TOOTH TOO.

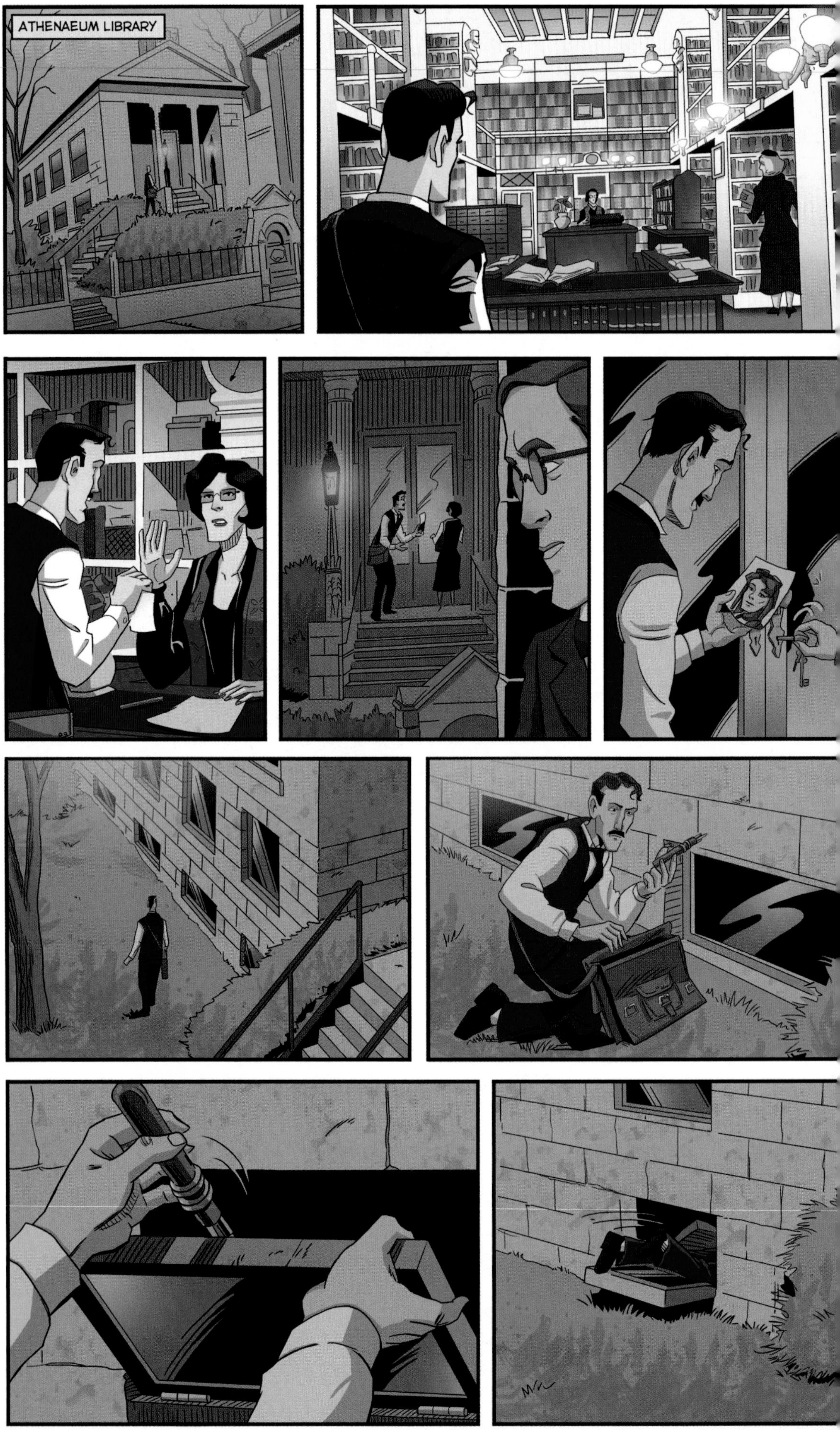
ATHENAEUM LIBRARY

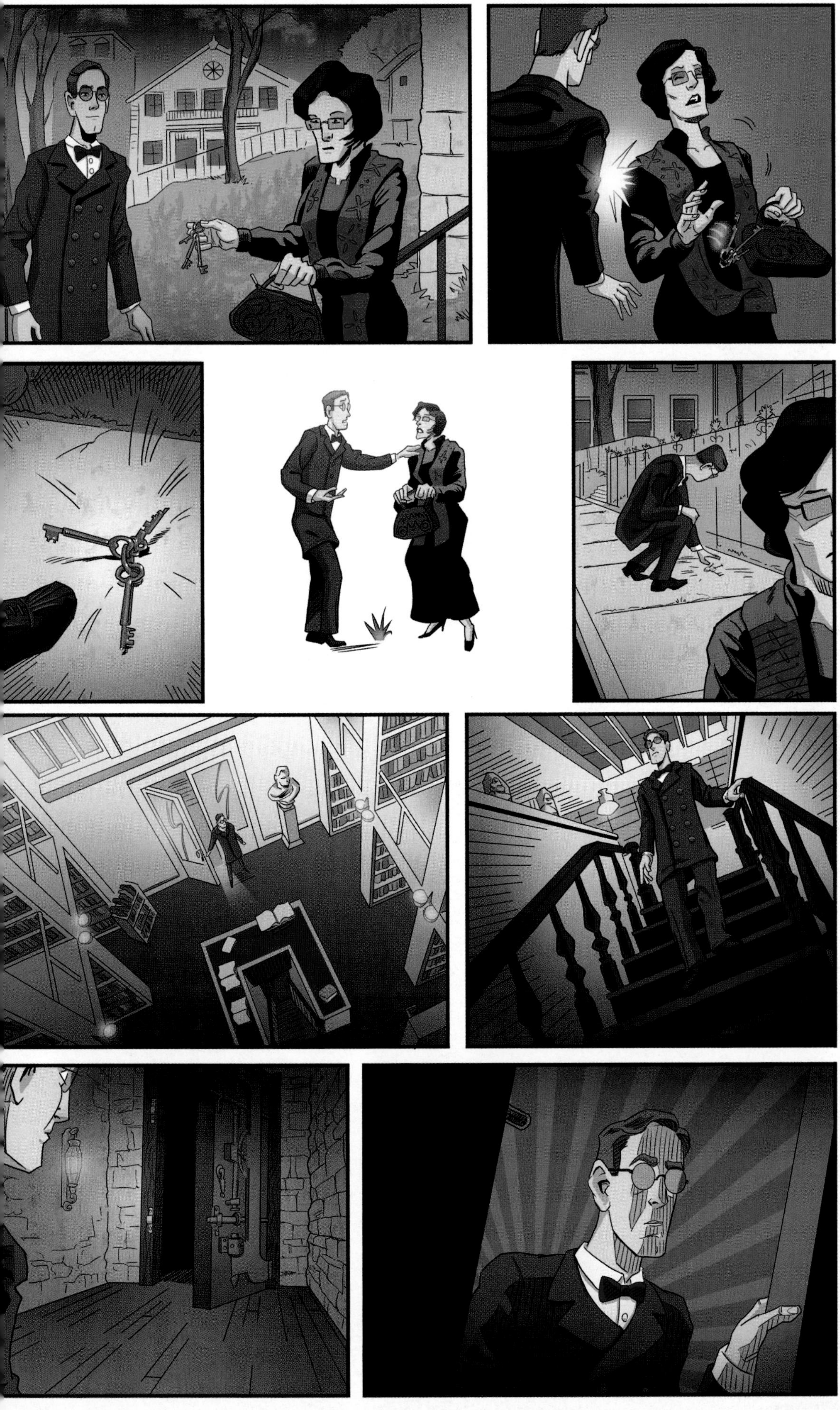

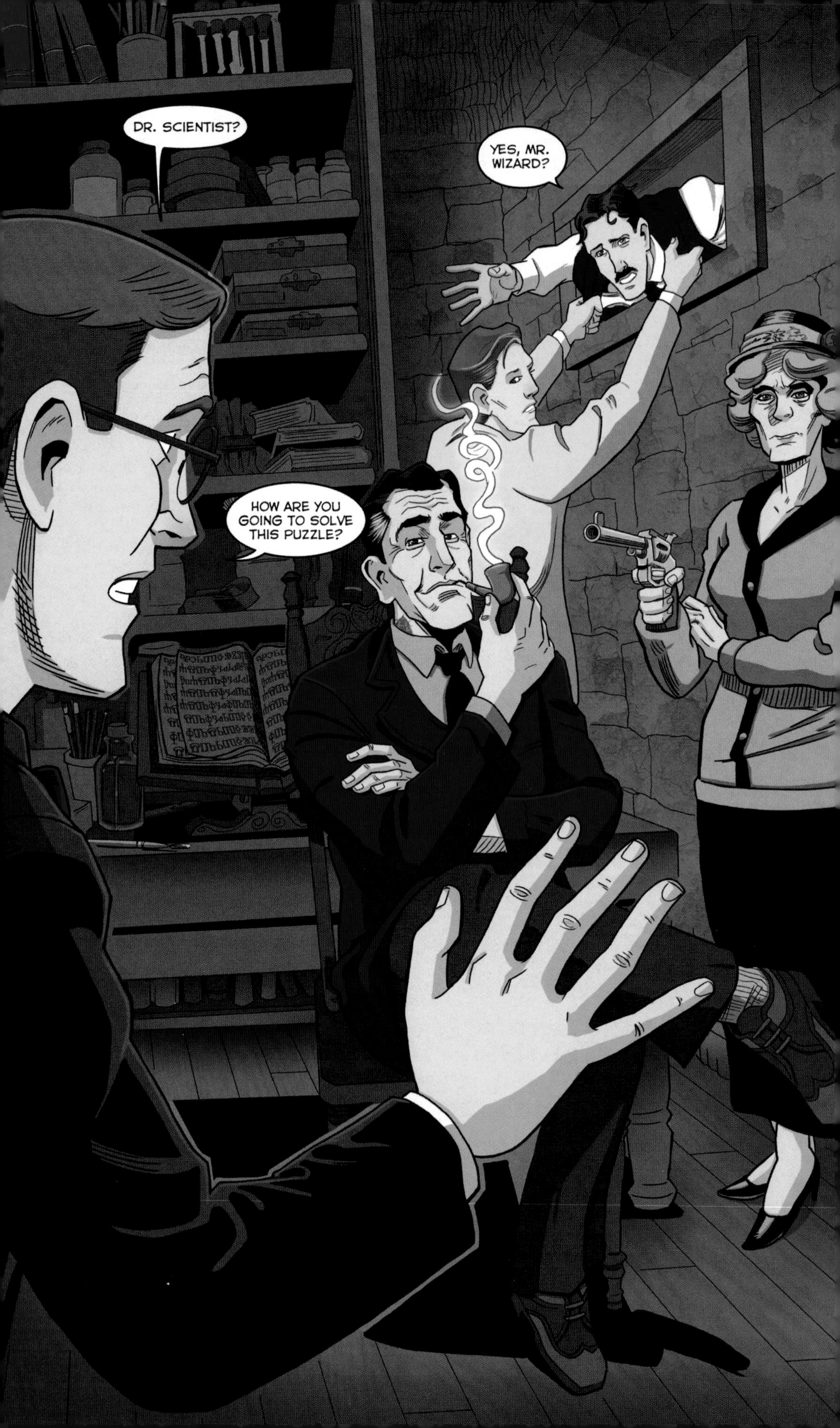
DR. SCIENTIST?
YES, MR. WIZARD?
HOW ARE YOU GOING TO SOLVE THIS PUZZLE?

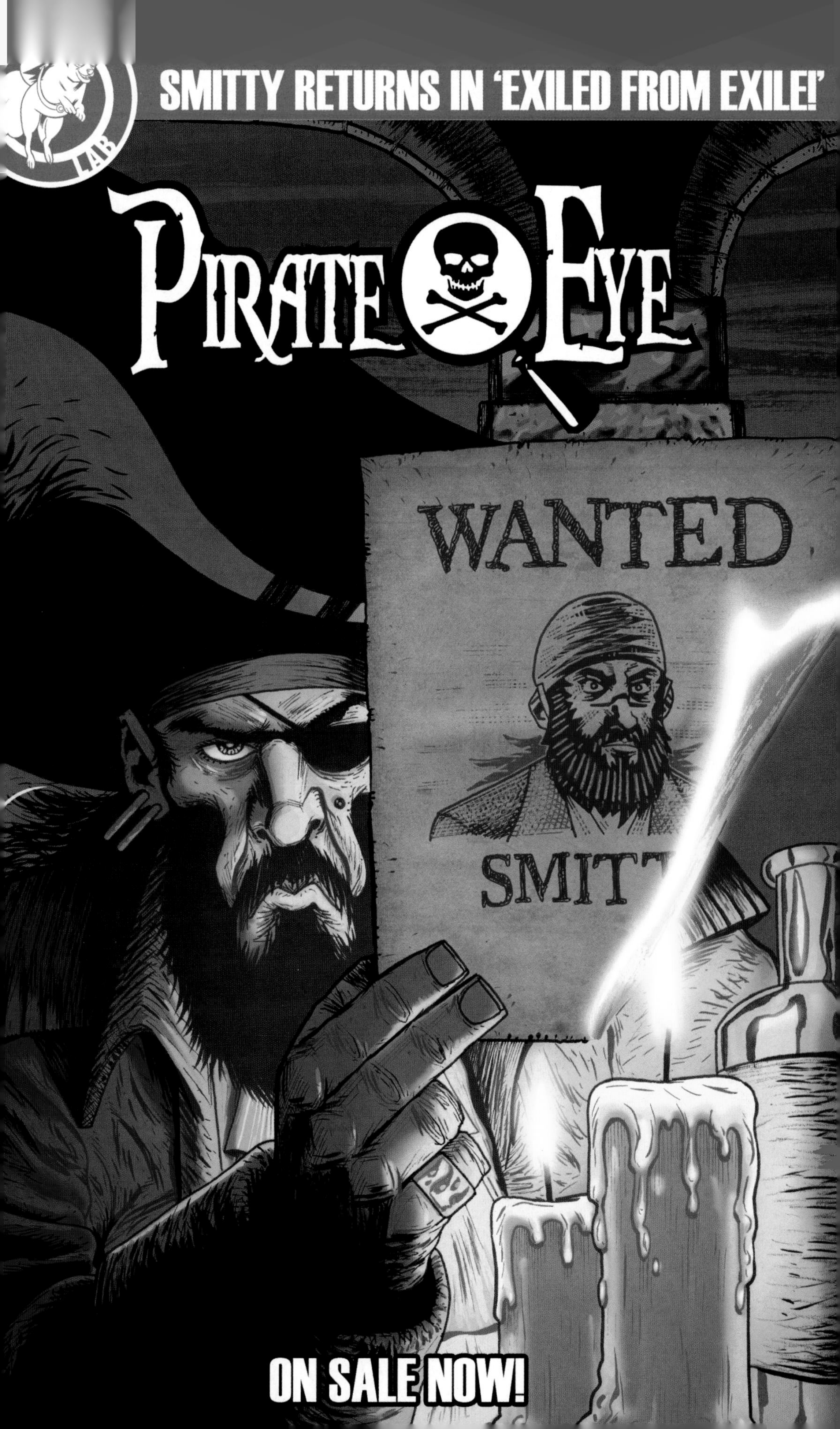
SMITTY RETURNS IN 'EXILED FROM EXILE!'
LAB
PIRATE EYE
WANTED
SMITT
ON SALE NOW!

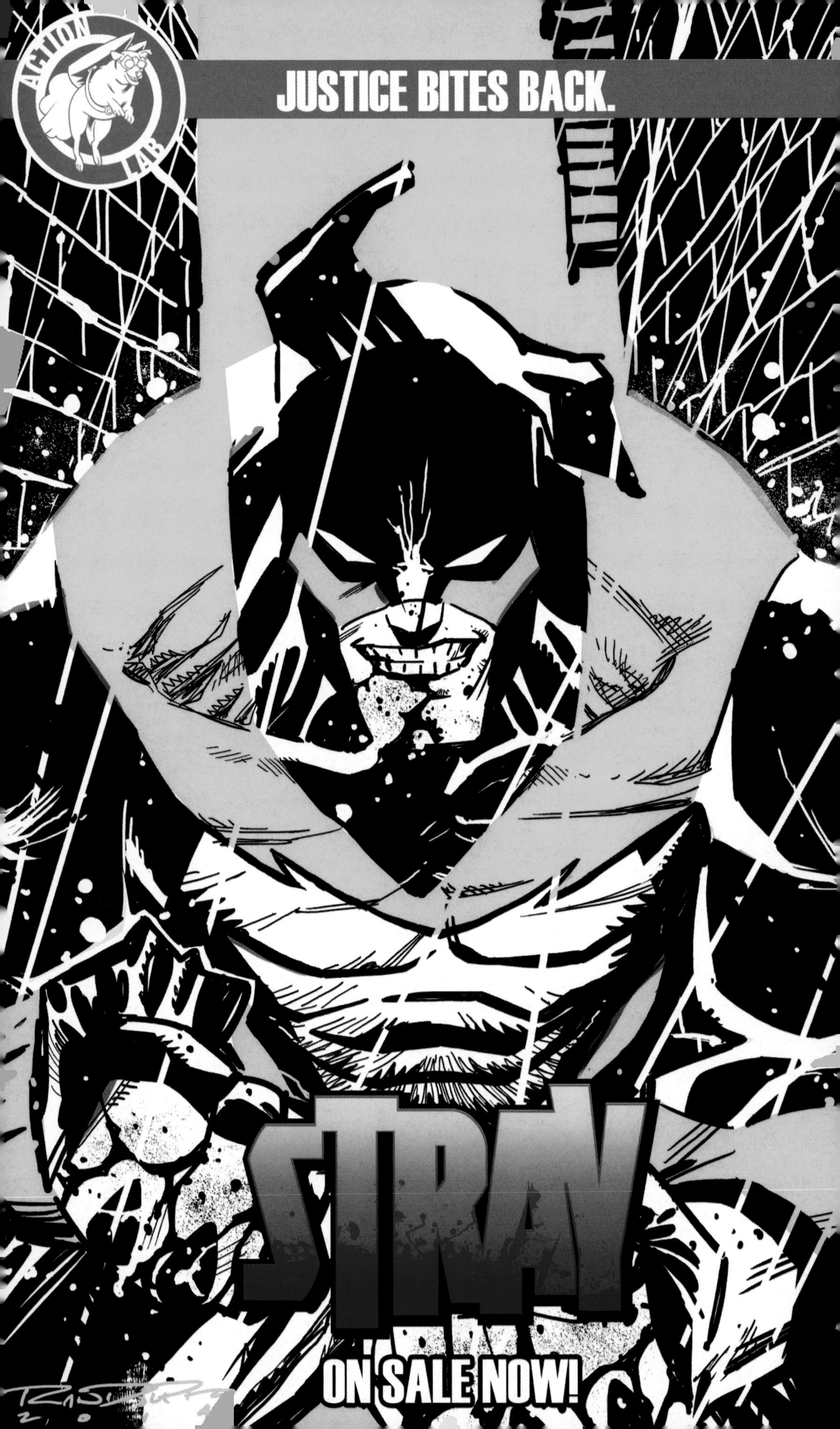
ACTION LAB
JUSTICE BITES BACK.
STRAY
ON SALE NOW!

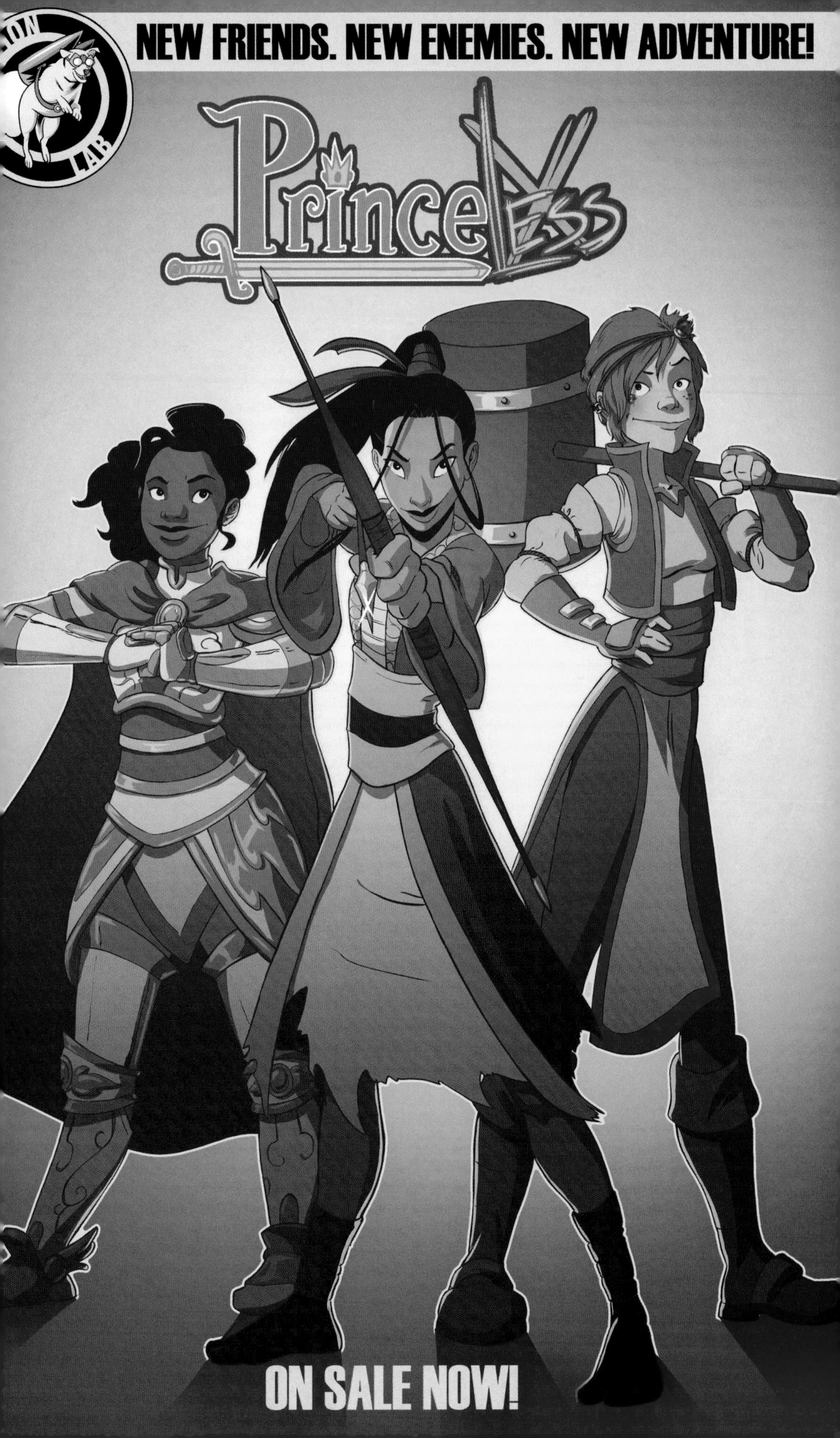
NEW FRIENDS. NEW ENEMIES. NEW ADVENTURE!
Princeless
ON SALE NOW!

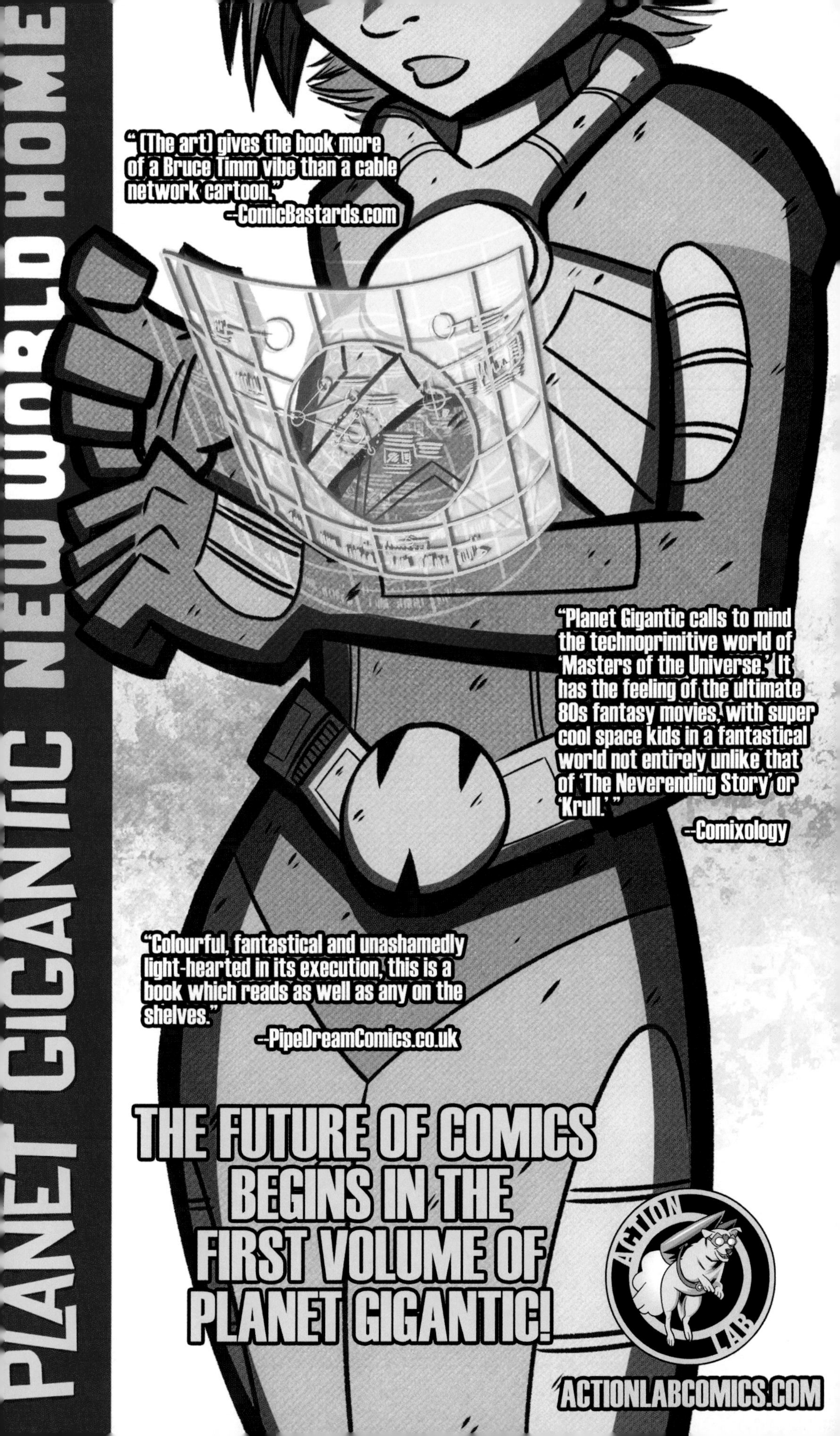

PLANET GIGANTIC NEW WORLD HOME
" (The art) gives the book more of a Bruce Timm vibe than a cable network cartoon."
--ComicBastards.com
"Planet Gigantic calls to mind the technoprimitive world of 'Masters of the Universe.' It has the feeling of the ultimate 80s fantasy movies, with super cool space kids in a fantastical world not entirely unlike that of 'The Neverending Story' or 'Krull.' "
--Comixology
"Colourful, fantastical and unashamedly light-hearted in its execution, this is a book which reads as well as any on the shelves."
--PipeDreamComics.co.uk
THE FUTURE OF COMICS BEGINS IN THE FIRST VOLUME OF PLANET GIGANTIC!
ACTION LAB
ACTIONLABCOMICS.COM

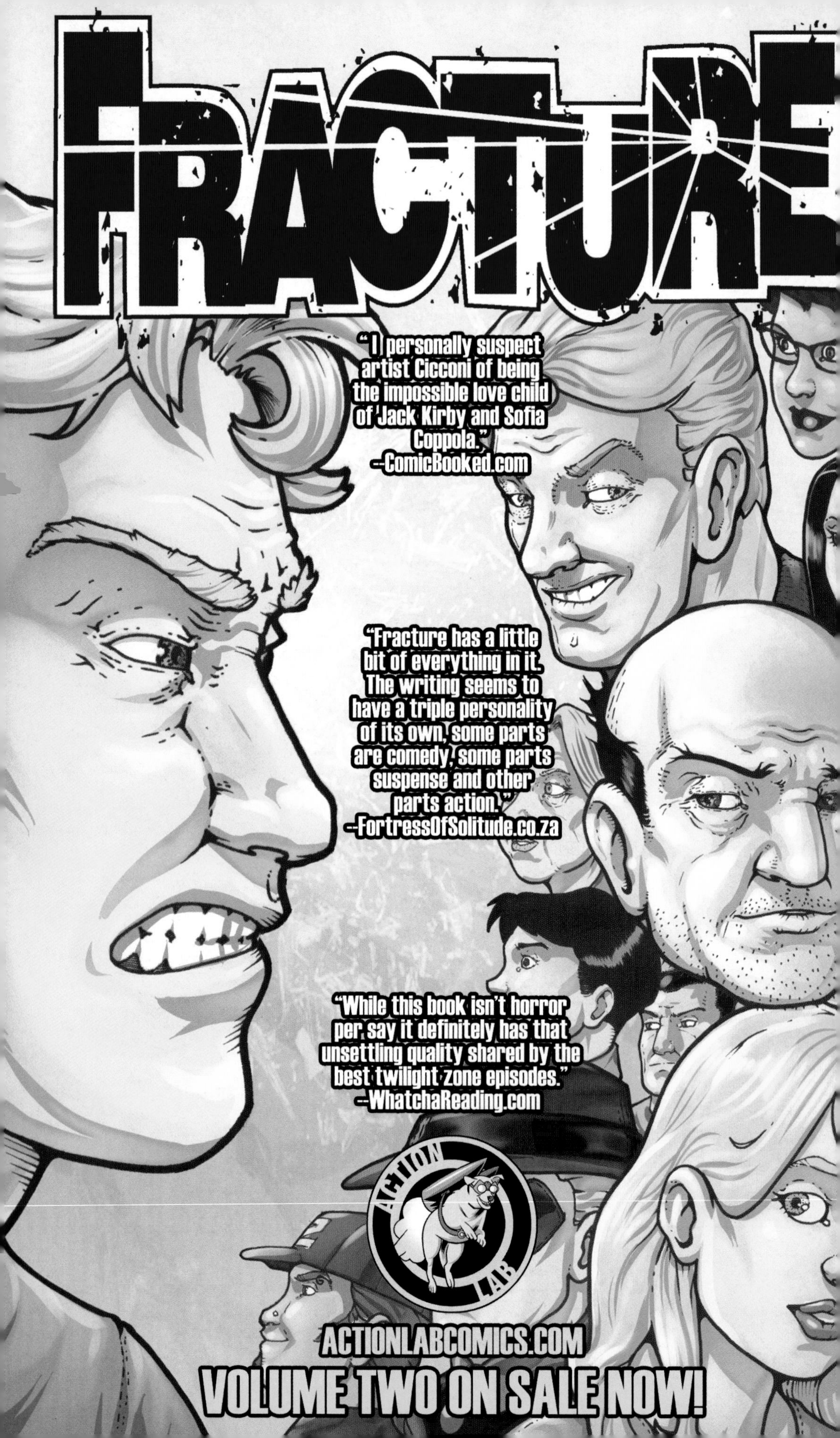
FRACTURE
"I personally suspect artist Cicconi of being the impossible love child of Jack Kirby and Sofia Coppola."
--ComicBooked.com
"Fracture has a little bit of everything in it. The writing seems to have a triple personality of its own, some parts are comedy, some parts suspense and other parts action."
--FortressOfSolitude.co.za
"While this book isn't horror per say it definitely has that unsettling quality shared by the best twilight zone episodes."
--WhatchaReading.com
ACTION LAB
ACTIONLABCOMICS.COM
VOLUME TWO ON SALE NOW!

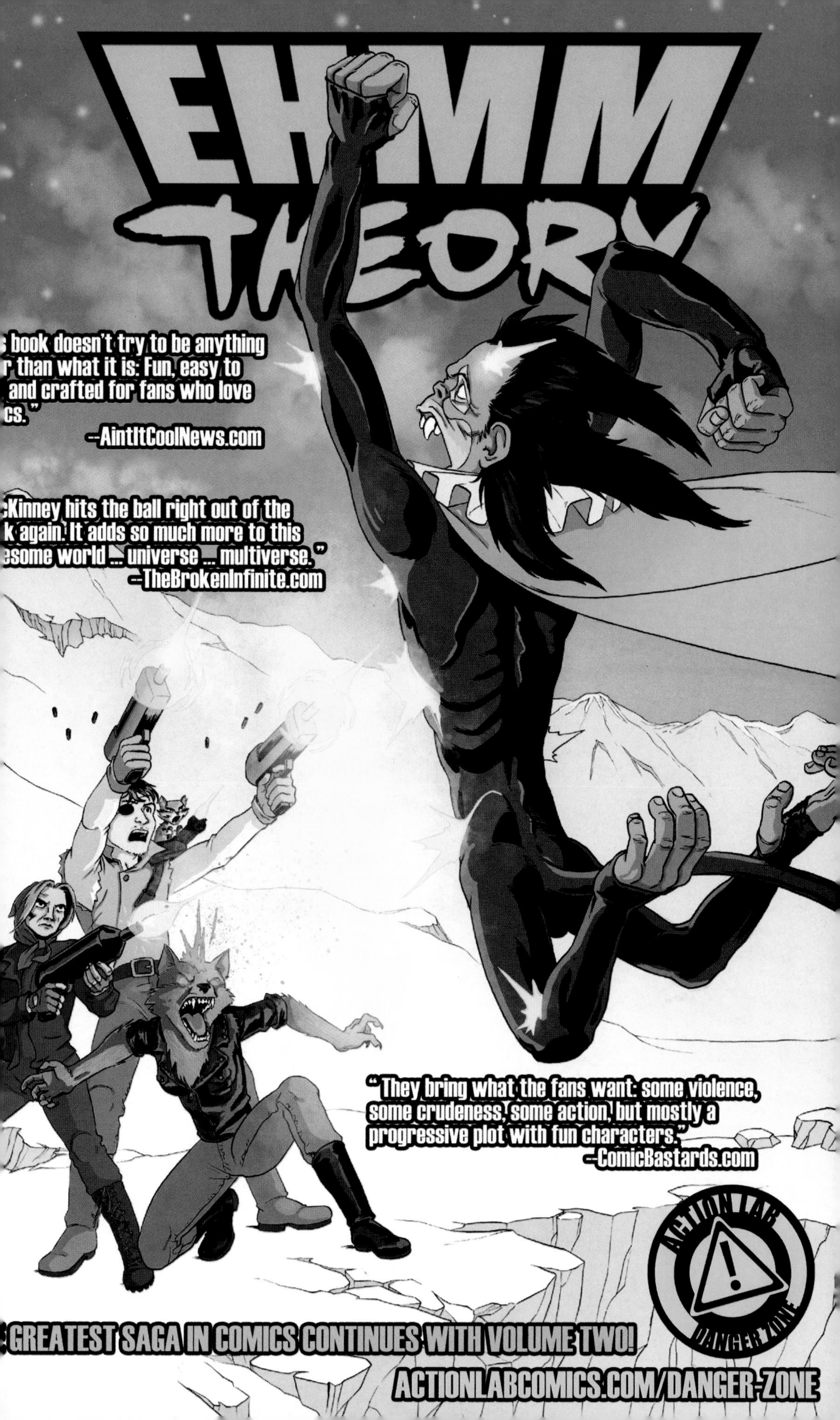

EHMM THEORY
s book doesn't try to be anything r than what it is: Fun, easy to and crafted for fans who love cs."
--AintItCoolNews.com
:Kinney hits the ball right out of the k again. It adds so much more to this esome world ... universe ... multiverse."
--TheBrokenInfinite.com
"They bring what the fans want: some violence, some crudeness, some action, but mostly a progressive plot with fun characters."
--ComicBastards.com
ACTION LAB
DANGER ZONE
GREATEST SAGA IN COMICS CONTINUES WITH VOLUME TWO!
ACTIONLABCOMICS.COM/DANGER-ZONE

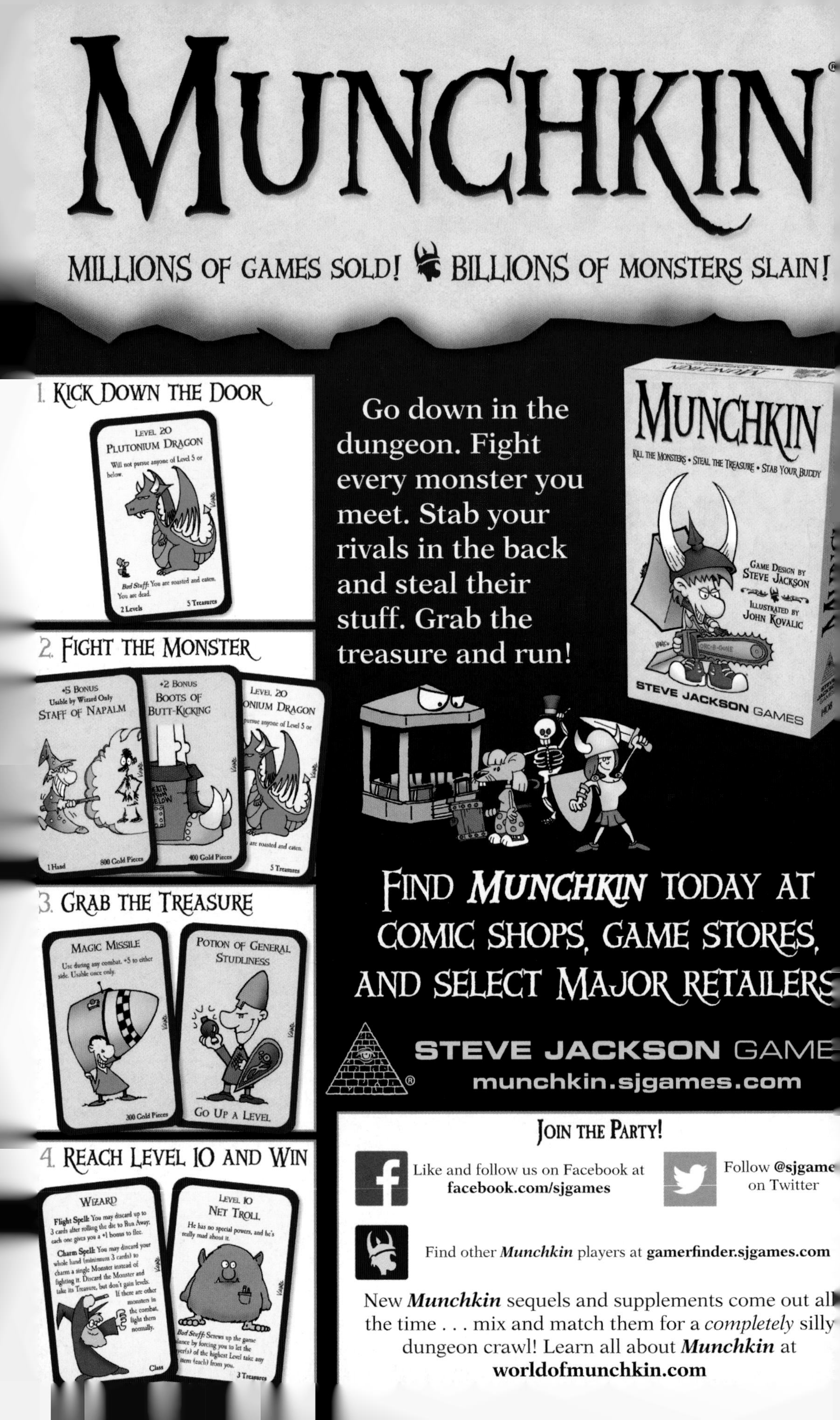
MUNCHKIN®
MILLIONS OF GAMES SOLD! BILLIONS OF MONSTERS SLAIN!
1. KICK DOWN THE DOOR
Level 20
Plutonium Dragon
Will not pursue anyone of Level 5 or below.
Bad Stuff: You are roasted and eaten. You are dead.
2 Levels
5 Treasures
2. FIGHT THE MONSTER
+5 Bonus
Usable by Wizard Only
Staff of Napalm
1 Hand
800 Gold Pieces
+2 Bonus
Boots of Butt-Kicking
400 Gold Pieces
3. GRAB THE TREASURE
Magic Missile
Use during any combat. +5 to either side. Usable once only.
300 Gold Pieces
Potion of General Studliness
Go Up a Level
4. REACH LEVEL 10 AND WIN
Wizard
Flight Spell: You may discard up to 3 cards after rolling the die to Run Away; each one gives you a +1 bonus to flee.
Charm Spell: You may discard your whole hand (minimum 3 cards) to charm a single Monster instead of fighting it. Discard the Monster and take its Treasure, but don't gain levels. If there are other monsters in the combat, fight them normally.
Class
Level 10
Net Troll
He has no special powers, and he's really mad about it.
3 Treasures
Go down in the dungeon. Fight every monster you meet. Stab your rivals in the back and steal their stuff. Grab the treasure and run!
MUNCHKIN
Kill the Monsters • Steal the Treasure • Stab Your Buddy
Game Design by Steve Jackson
Illustrated by John Kovalic
STEVE JACKSON GAMES
FIND MUNCHKIN TODAY AT COMIC SHOPS, GAME STORES, AND SELECT MAJOR RETAILERS
STEVE JACKSON GAMES
munchkin.sjgames.com
JOIN THE PARTY!
Like and follow us on Facebook at facebook.com/sjgames
Follow @sjgames on Twitter
Find other Munchkin players at gamerfinder.sjgames.com
New Munchkin sequels and supplements come out all the time . . . mix and match them for a completely silly dungeon crawl! Learn all about Munchkin at worldofmunchkin.com

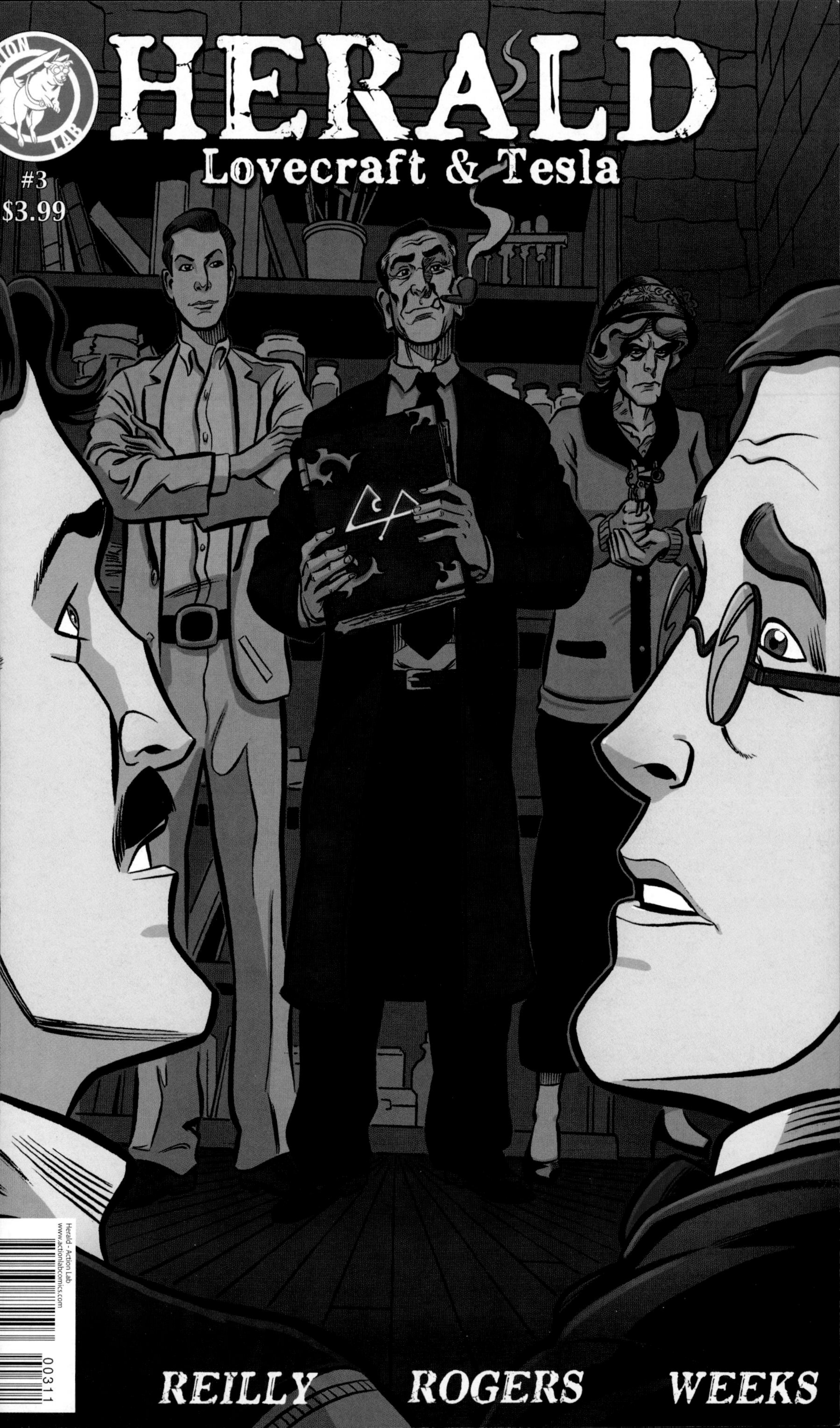
HERALD
Lovecraft & Tesla
#3
$3.99
Herald - Action Lab
www.actionlabcomics.com
00311
REILLY
ROGERS
WEEKS

זּERALD
Lovecraft & Tesla

History in the Making
Issue 3 of 3

Written by **John Reilly**

Pencils and Page 10-22 inks by **Tom Rogers**

Ink, Color, Letters by **Dexter Weeks**

Logo Design by **Michelle Nikolajevic**

Action Lab Comics

Publisher - **Bryan Seaton**   President - **Kevin Freeman**   Creative Director - **Dave Dwonch**

Editor-in-Chief - **Shawn Gabborin**   Co-Directors of Marketing - **Jamal Igle & Kelly Dale**

Social Media Director - **Jim Dietz**   Education Outreach Director - **Jeremey Whitley**

Associate Editors - **Chad Cicconi & Colleen Boyd**

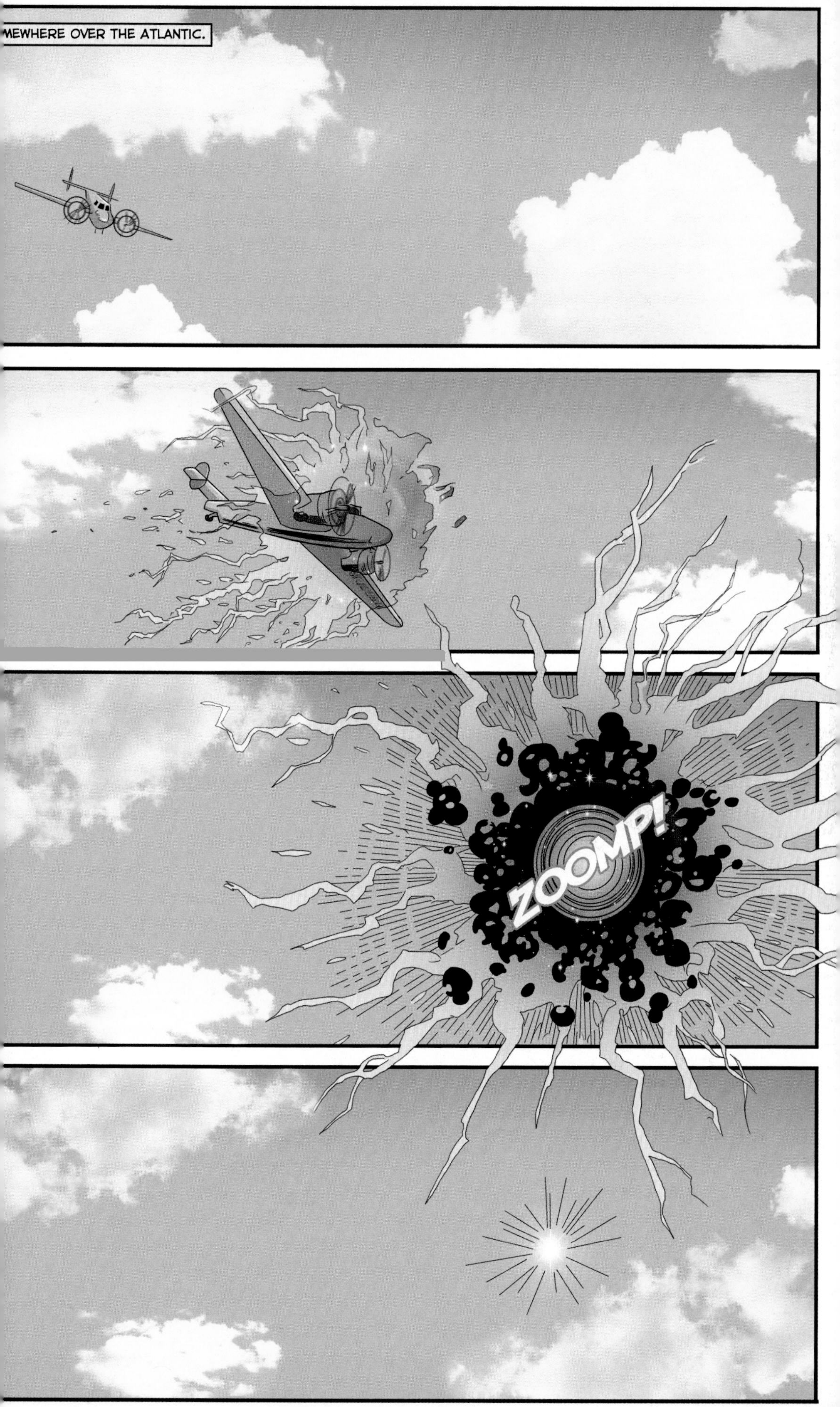
MEWHERE OVER THE ATLANTIC.
ZOOMP!

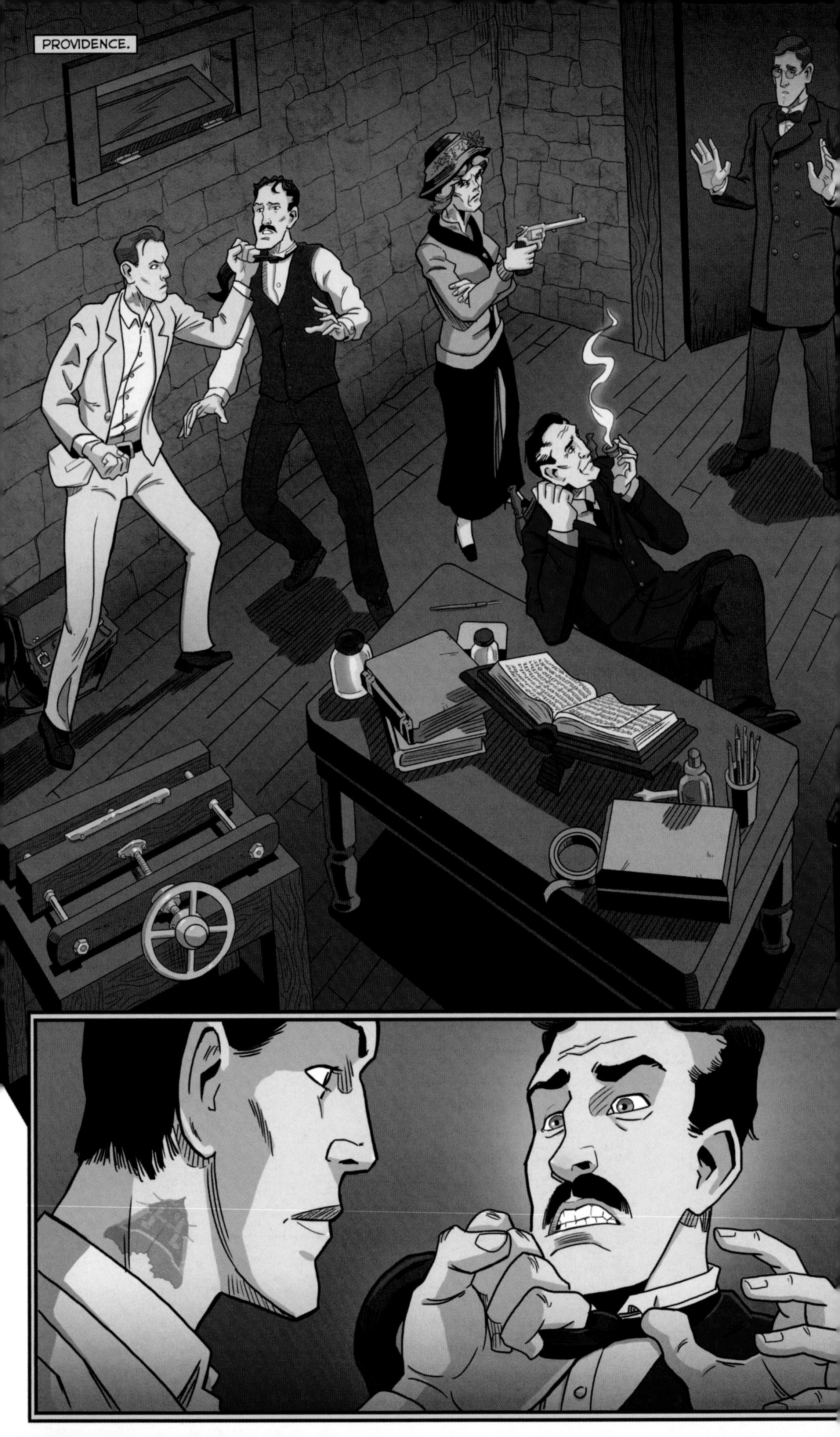
PROVIDENCE.

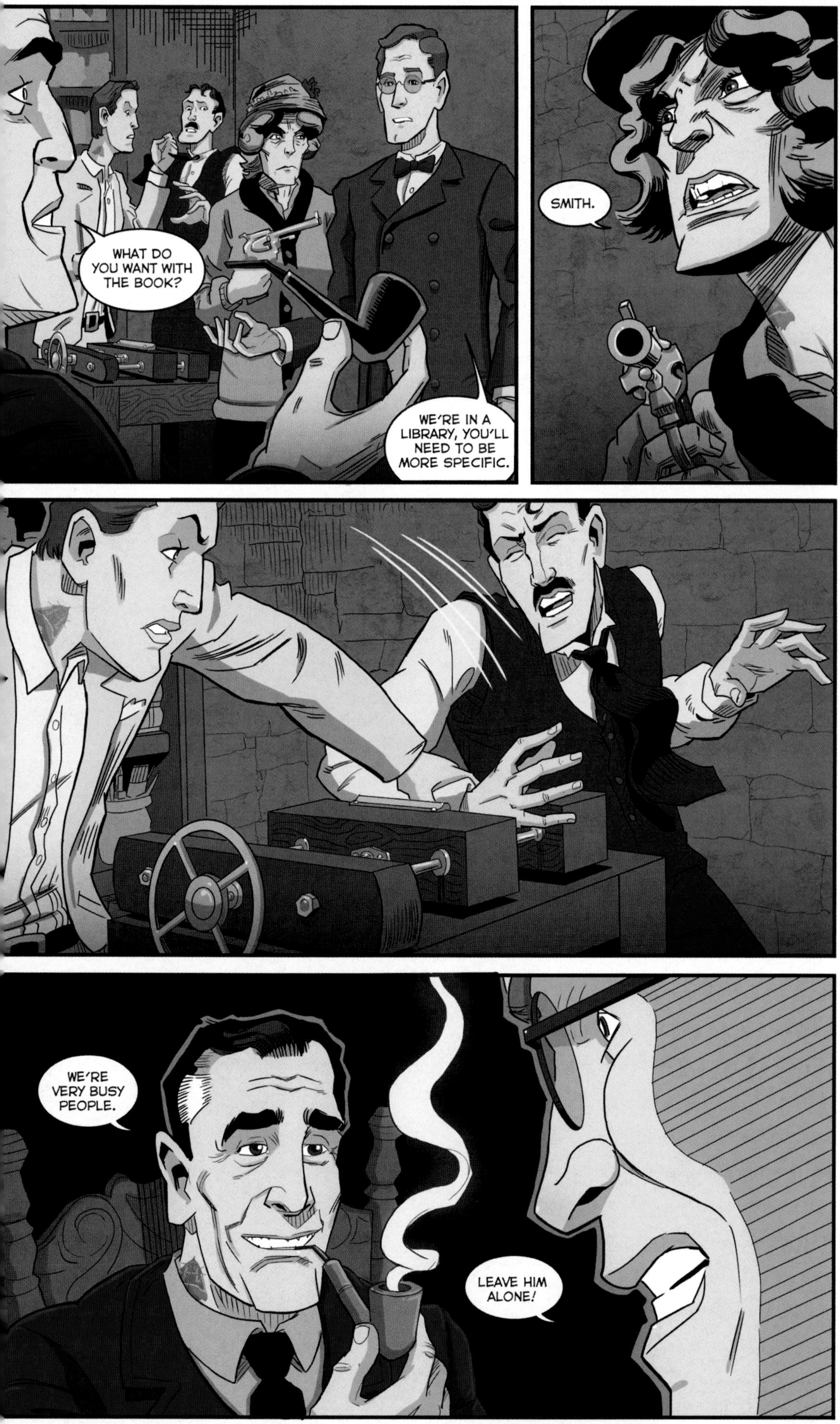
WHAT DO YOU WANT WITH THE BOOK?
WE'RE IN A LIBRARY, YOU'LL NEED TO BE MORE SPECIFIC.
SMITH.
WE'RE VERY BUSY PEOPLE.
LEAVE HIM ALONE!

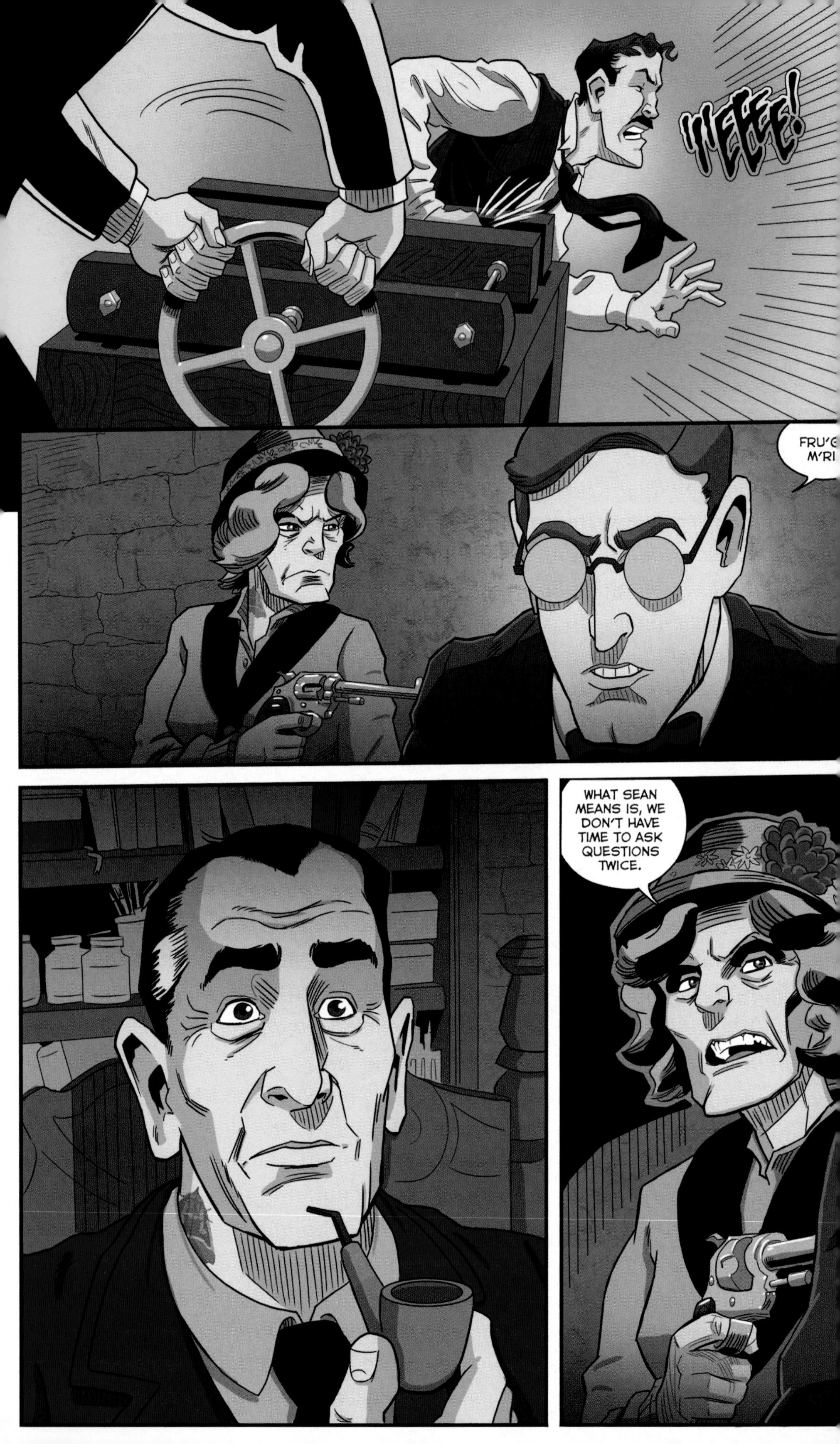

WEEEE!
FRU'G
M'RI
WHAT SEAN MEANS IS, WE DON'T HAVE TIME TO ASK QUESTIONS TWICE.

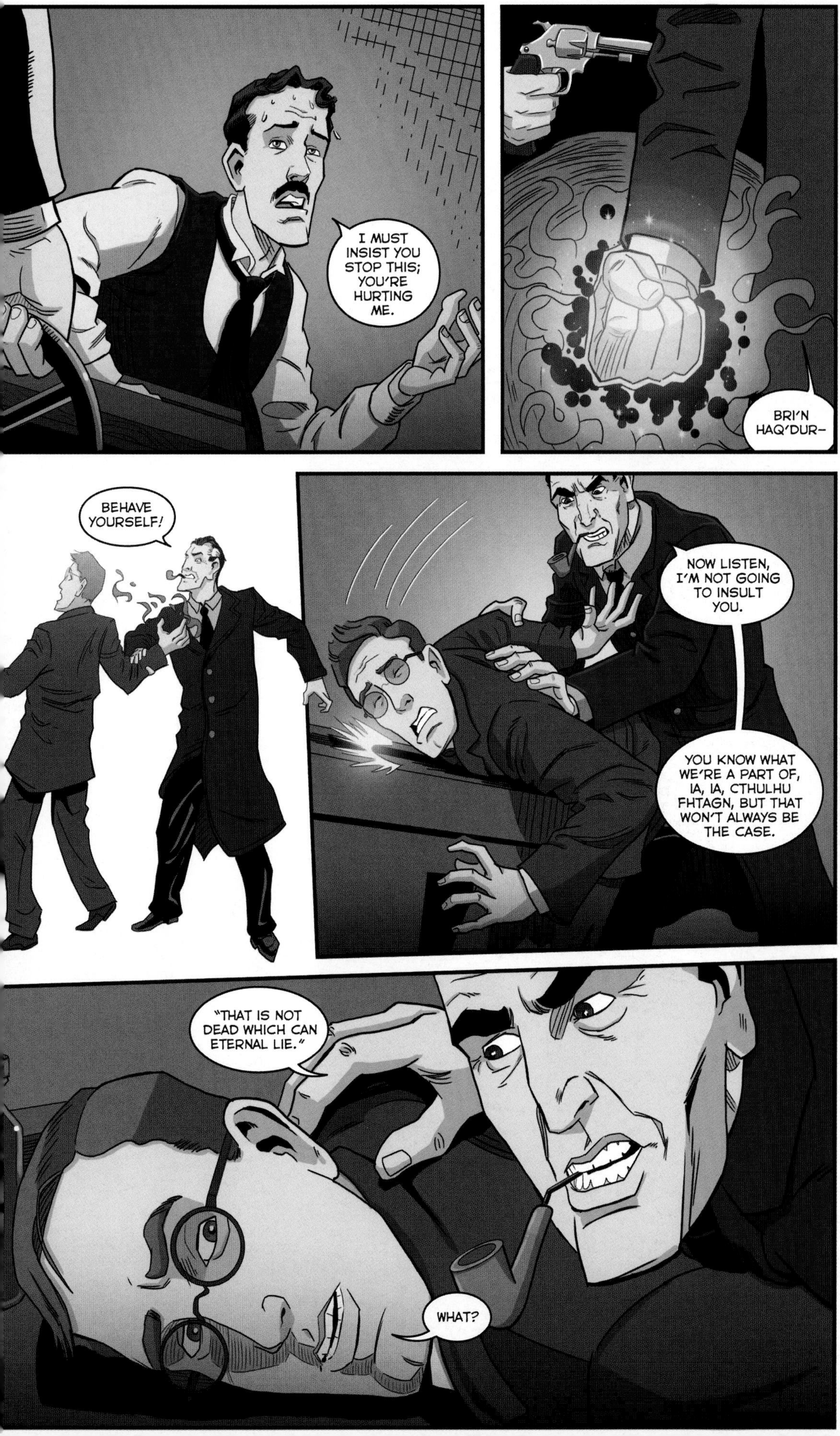
I MUST INSIST YOU STOP THIS; YOU'RE HURTING ME.
BRI'N HAQ'DUR–
BEHAVE YOURSELF!
NOW LISTEN, I'M NOT GOING TO INSULT YOU.
YOU KNOW WHAT WE'RE A PART OF, IA, IA, CTHULHU FHTAGN, BUT THAT WON'T ALWAYS BE THE CASE.
"THAT IS NOT DEAD WHICH CAN ETERNAL LIE."
WHAT?

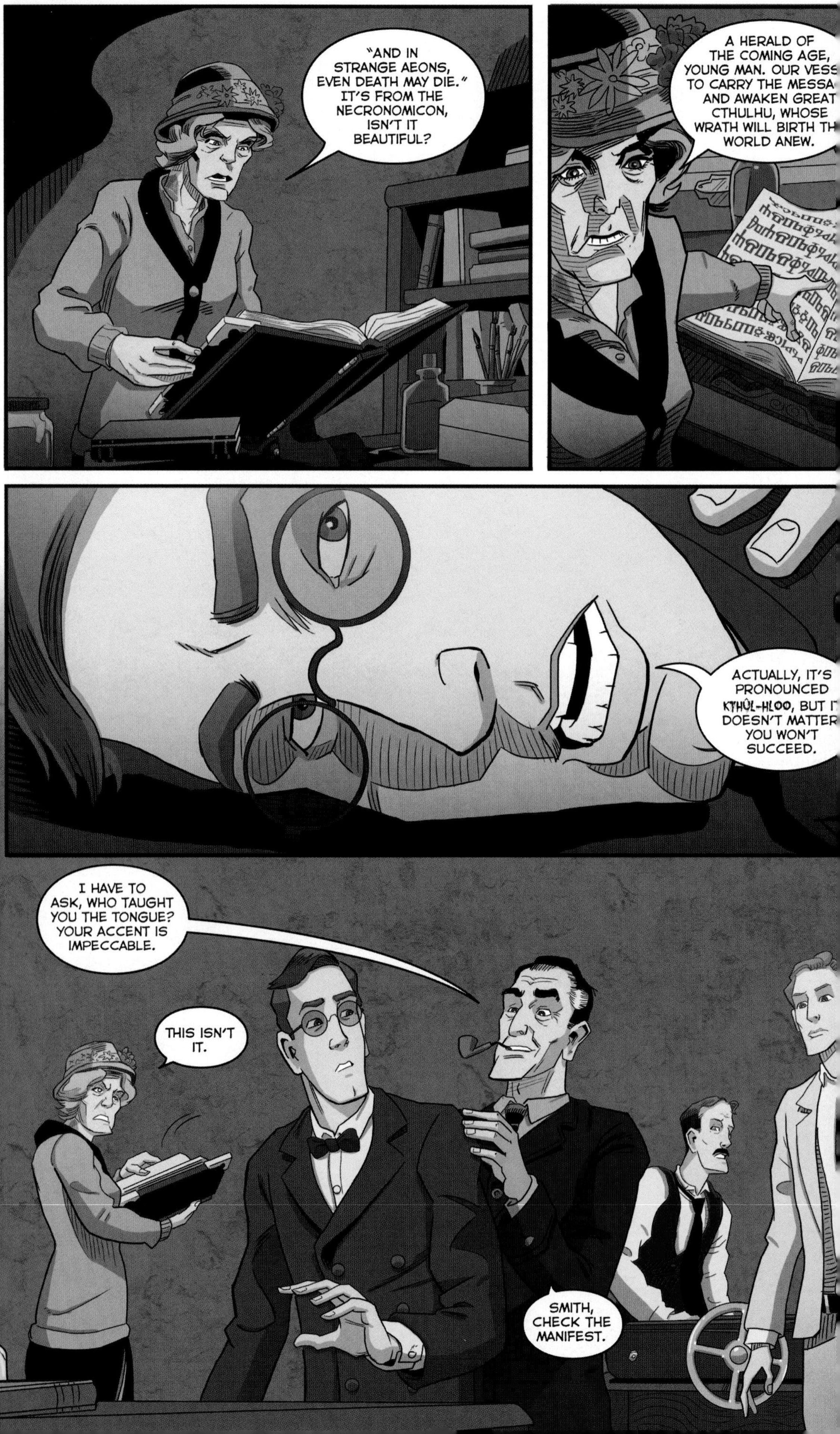
"AND IN STRANGE AEONS, EVEN DEATH MAY DIE." IT'S FROM THE NECRONOMICON, ISN'T IT BEAUTIFUL?
A HERALD OF THE COMING AGE, YOUNG MAN. OUR VESS TO CARRY THE MESSA AND AWAKEN GREAT CTHULHU, WHOSE WRATH WILL BIRTH TH WORLD ANEW.
ACTUALLY, IT'S PRONOUNCED KTHÛL-HLOO, BUT IT DOESN'T MATTER YOU WON'T SUCCEED.
I HAVE TO ASK, WHO TAUGHT YOU THE TONGUE? YOUR ACCENT IS IMPECCABLE.
THIS ISN'T IT.
SMITH, CHECK THE MANIFEST.

I DON'T GIVE A *DAMN* WHAT THE MANIFEST SAYS, THIS IS A FORGERY!

EASY, MATILDA, OTHERS WERE SOLD AT THE AUCTION. WE'LL FIND AN ORIGINAL SOON ENOUGH.

MR. LOVECRAFT, WHO *ARE* THESE PEOPLE?

THESE ARE THE BAD GUYS, DOC.

YOU CAN RECOGNIZE THEM BY THE MOTH TATTOOS ON THEIR NECKS—

—AND THE INSANE SPEECHES THEY MAKE ABOUT IMPROVING THE WORLD BY DESTROYING IT.

THEY'RE ALSO GRAVELY MISGUIDED IN BELIEVING ANY ORIGINAL COPIES OF THE NECRONOMICON STILL EXIST.

EVEN PROFESSOR CARLOW KNOWS *THAT*.

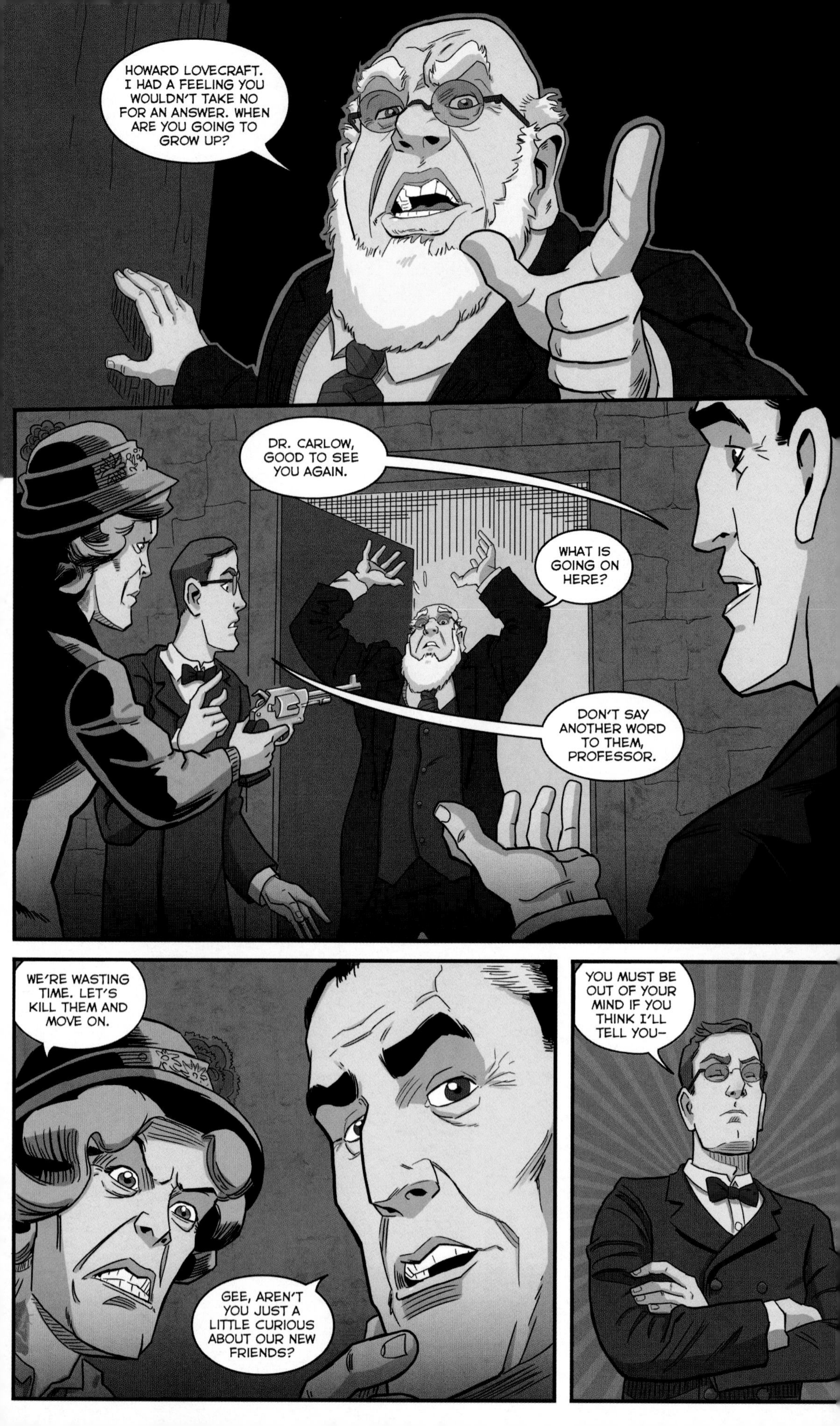
HOWARD LOVECRAFT. I HAD A FEELING YOU WOULDN'T TAKE NO FOR AN ANSWER. WHEN ARE YOU GOING TO GROW UP?
DR. CARLOW, GOOD TO SEE YOU AGAIN.
WHAT IS GOING ON HERE?
DON'T SAY ANOTHER WORD TO THEM, PROFESSOR.
WE'RE WASTING TIME. LET'S KILL THEM AND MOVE ON.
GEE, AREN'T YOU JUST A LITTLE CURIOUS ABOUT OUR NEW FRIENDS?
YOU MUST BE OUT OF YOUR MIND IF YOU THINK I'LL TELL YOU–

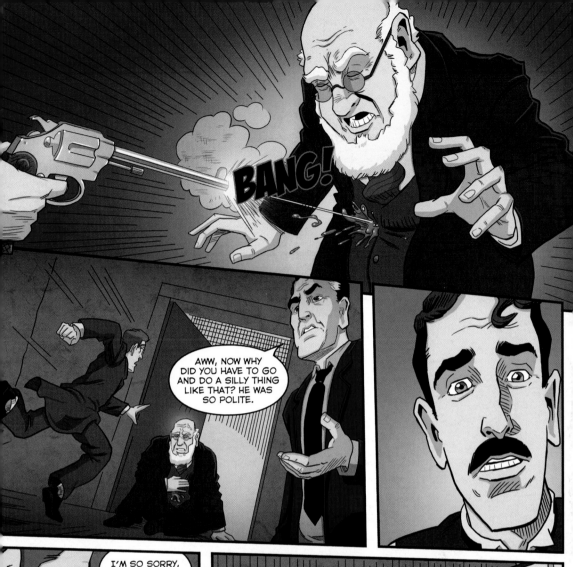

BANG!

AWW, NOW WHY DID YOU HAVE TO GO AND DO A SILLY THING LIKE THAT? HE WAS SO POLITE.

I'M SO SORRY, SYDNEY. I AM SO SORRY.

WHO ARE THESE PEOPLE?

WE'RE THE BAD GUYS, DOC.

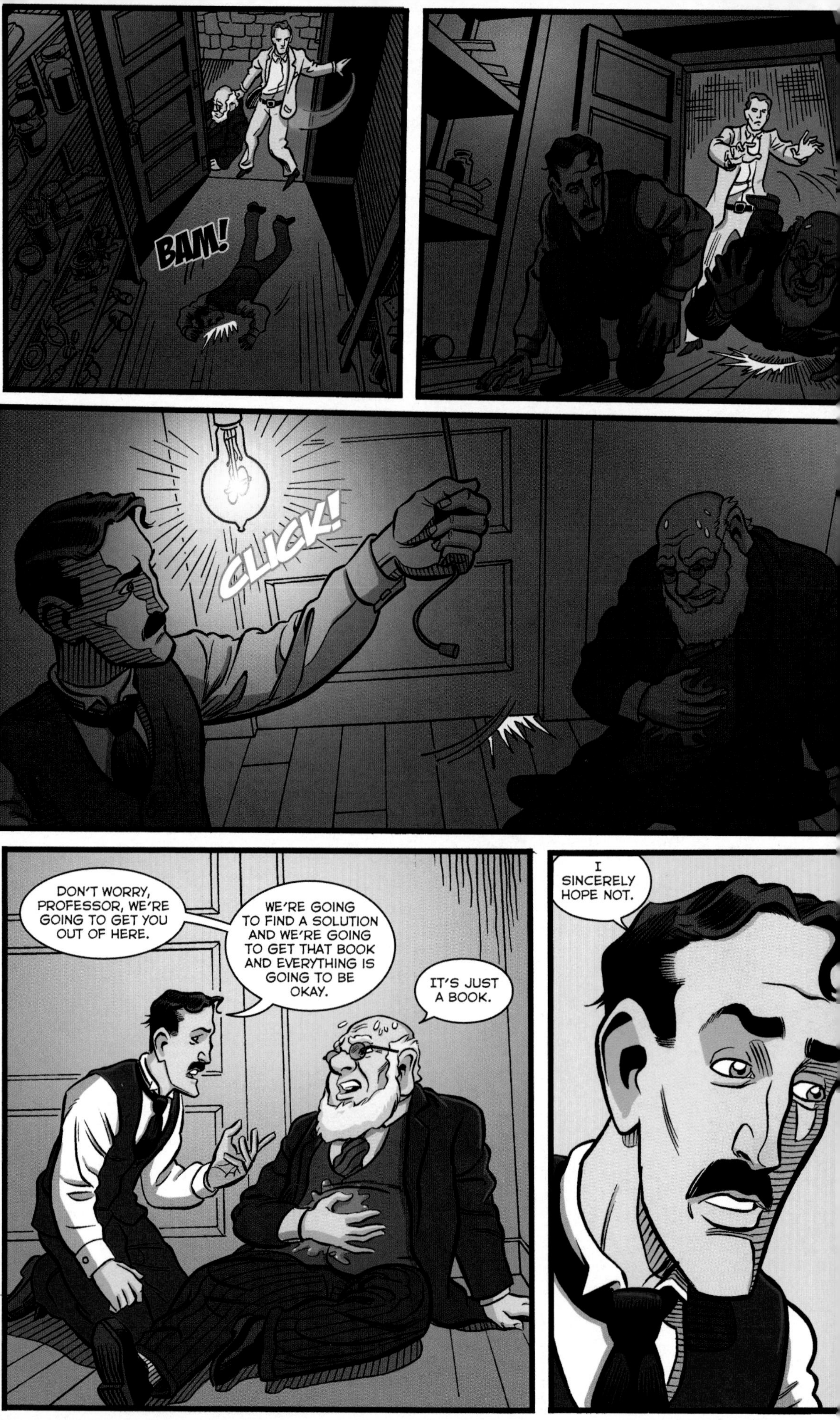
BAM!
CLICK!
DON'T WORRY, PROFESSOR, WE'RE GOING TO GET YOU OUT OF HERE.
WE'RE GOING TO FIND A SOLUTION AND WE'RE GOING TO GET THAT BOOK AND EVERYTHING IS GOING TO BE OKAY.
IT'S JUST A BOOK.
I SINCERELY HOPE NOT.

LOVE, I'M AFRAID.

WHAT DO YOU MEAN? IS THIS ABOUT MONEY?

I DON'T UNDERSTAND.

Potassium Aluminum Sulfate

NEITHER DO I, BUT IF PEOPLE ARE WILLING TO HURT OTHERS FOR THAT BOOK, THEN MAYBE IT *CAN* SAVE HER.

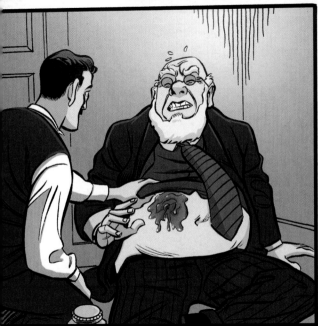

PLEASE HELP ME OPEN THIS. IT WILL HELP STOP THE BLEEDING, BUT YOU *WILL* FEEL SOME DISCOMFORT.

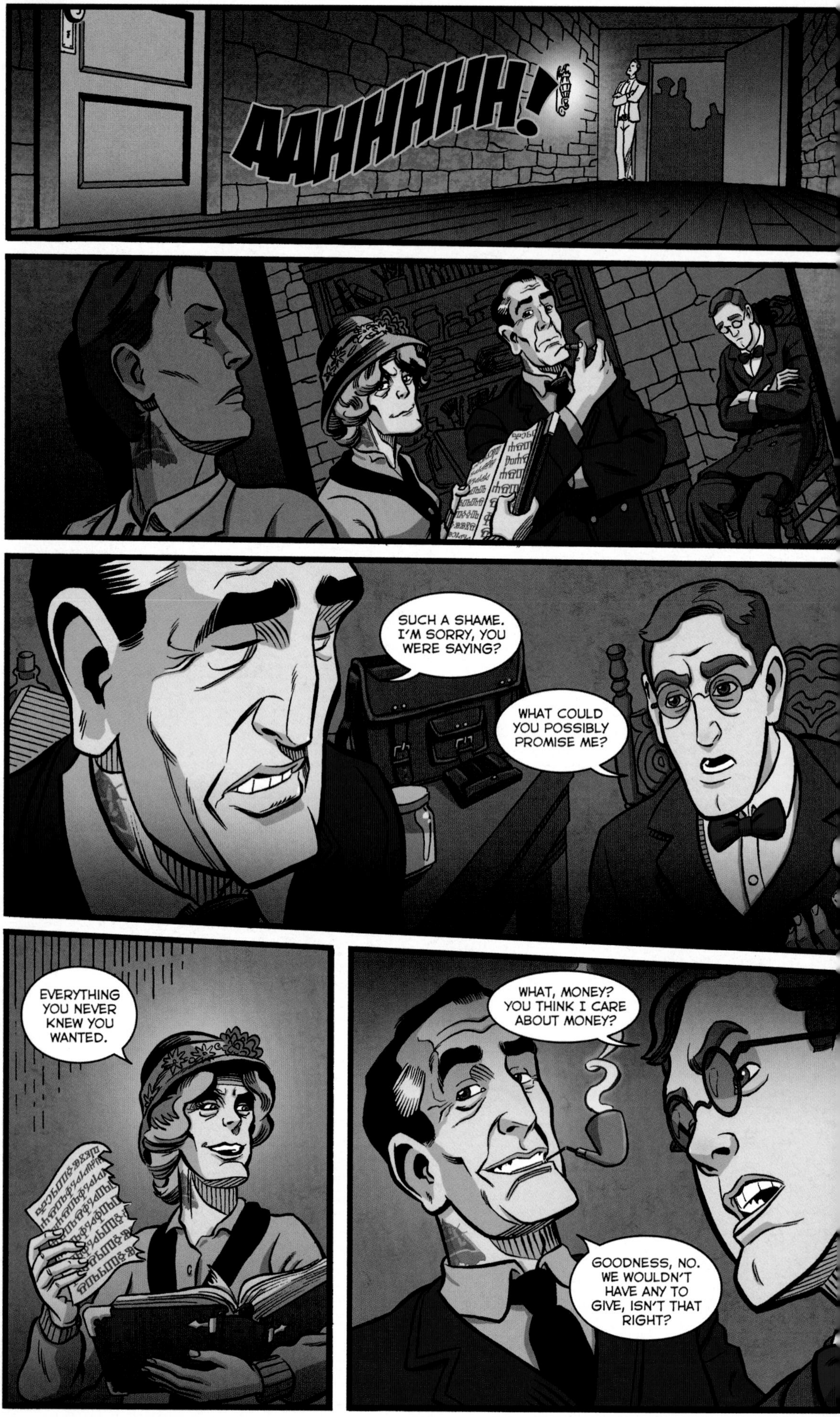
AAHHHHH!
SUCH A SHAME. I'M SORRY, YOU WERE SAYING?
WHAT COULD YOU POSSIBLY PROMISE ME?
EVERYTHING YOU NEVER KNEW YOU WANTED.
WHAT, MONEY? YOU THINK I CARE ABOUT MONEY?
GOODNESS, NO. WE WOULDN'T HAVE ANY TO GIVE, ISN'T THAT RIGHT?

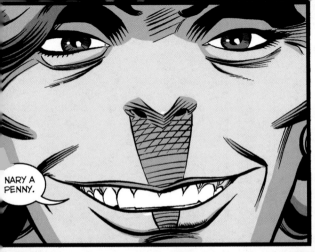

NARY A PENNY.

WHAT, THEN?

MR. LOVECRAFT, WHEN YOU WALK THE STREETS AND LOOK ON THE CURRENT STATE OF HUMANITY, WHAT DO YOU SEE?

I SUPPOSE WHAT *EVERYONE* SEES, A USELESS CACOPHONY OF EPICUREAN MEAT PUPPETS—

EXACTLY!

—NONE OF WHOM DESERVE TO BE SHOT IN THE GUT LIKE A WILD ANIMAL!

ONE LAST THING, SPORT. I'M CURIOUS, HOW ARE YOU ABLE TO SEE OUR MARKINGS? ONLY FOLKS WHO'VE JOINED THE FAMILY CAN SEE THESE.

WE ARE FAR FROM MY AREA OF EXPERTISE, BUT I'M SURE WE CAN FIND SOMETHING.

YOU MUST REALLY LOVE HER, HUH?

I CONSTRUCTED HER ENGAGEMENT RING BY HAND—A VERY SMALL RESONANT TRANSFORMER CIRCUIT. IT WORKS, TOO.

WHAT A LUCKY WOMAN. I NEVER MARRIED. NEVER SAW A REASON.

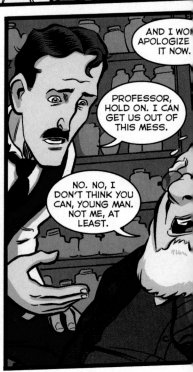

AND I WON APOLOGIZE IT NOW.

PROFESSOR, HOLD ON. I CAN GET US OUT OF THIS MESS.

NO. NO, I DON'T THINK YOU CAN, YOUNG MAN. NOT ME, AT LEAST.

HE CAN BE A HANDFUL, BUT HE'S A GOOD KID. IF YOU SEE HIM, TELL HIM IT'S NOT HIS FAULT.

AND WHEN YOU SEE THAT GIRL OF YOURS AGAIN, TELL HER...

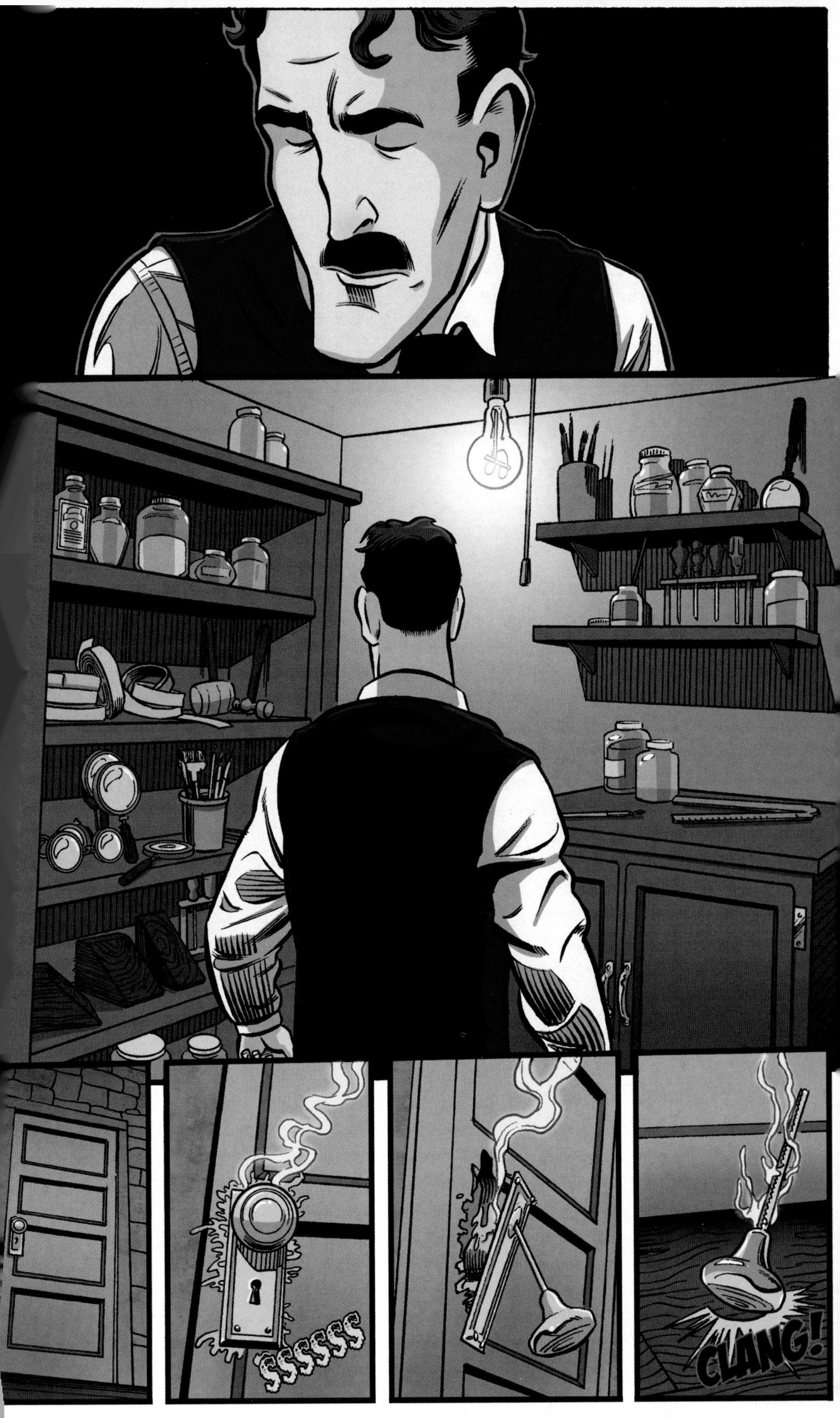
SSSSSS
CLANG!

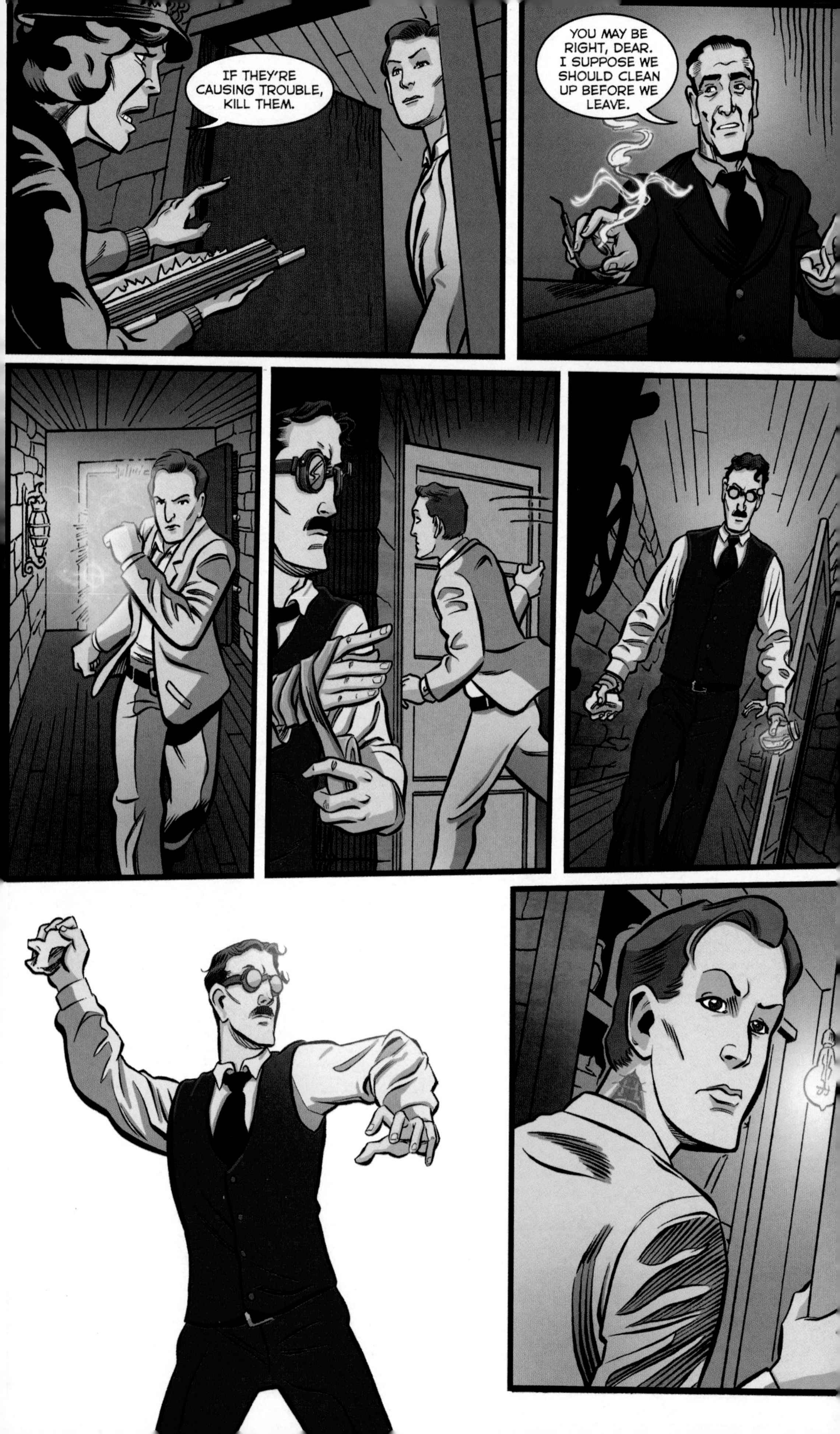
IF THEY'RE CAUSING TROUBLE, KILL THEM.
YOU MAY BE RIGHT, DEAR. I SUPPOSE WE SHOULD CLEAN UP BEFORE WE LEAVE.

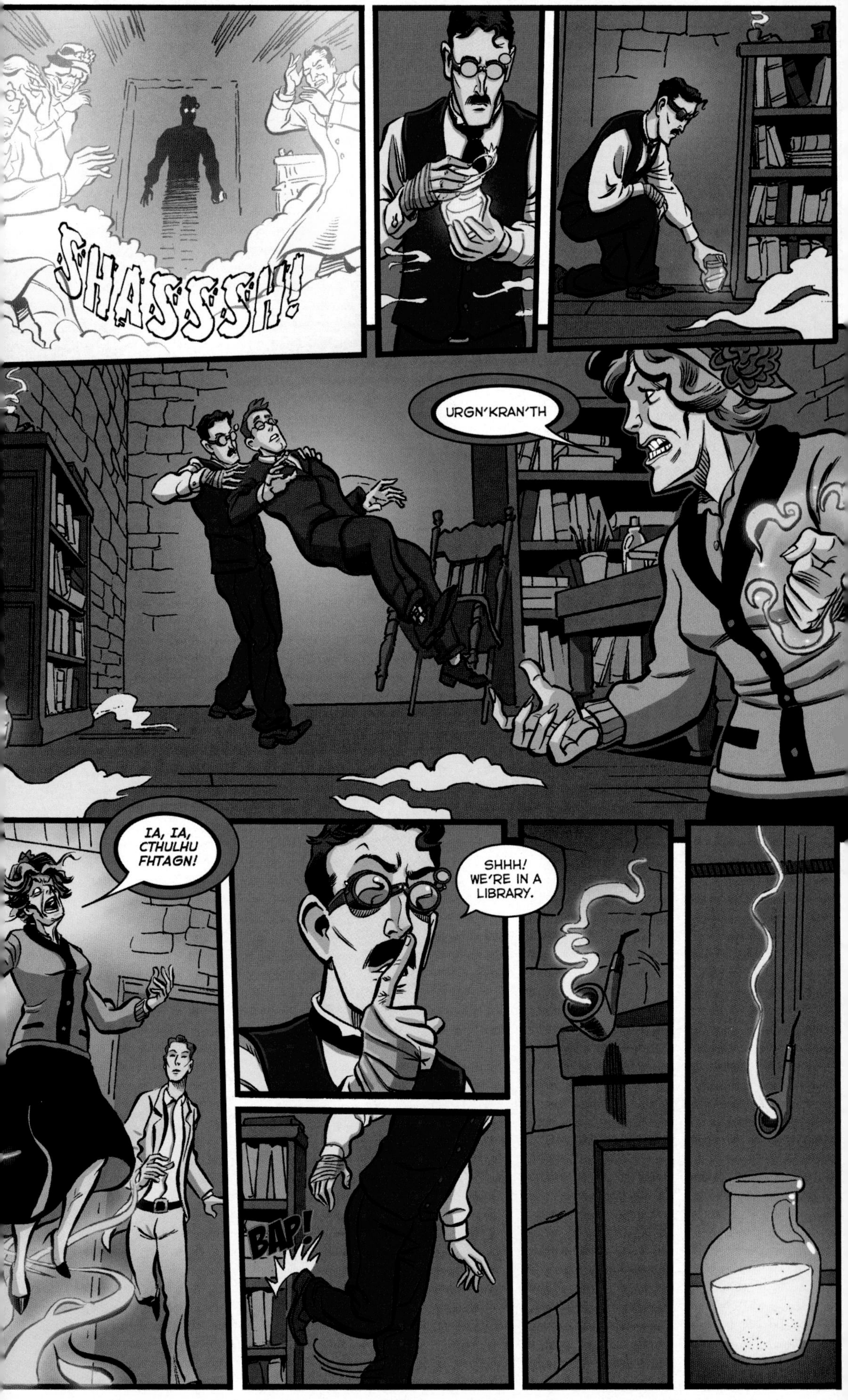
SHASSSH!
URGN'KRAN'TH
IA, IA, CTHULHU FHTAGN!
SHHH! WE'RE IN A LIBRARY.
BAP!

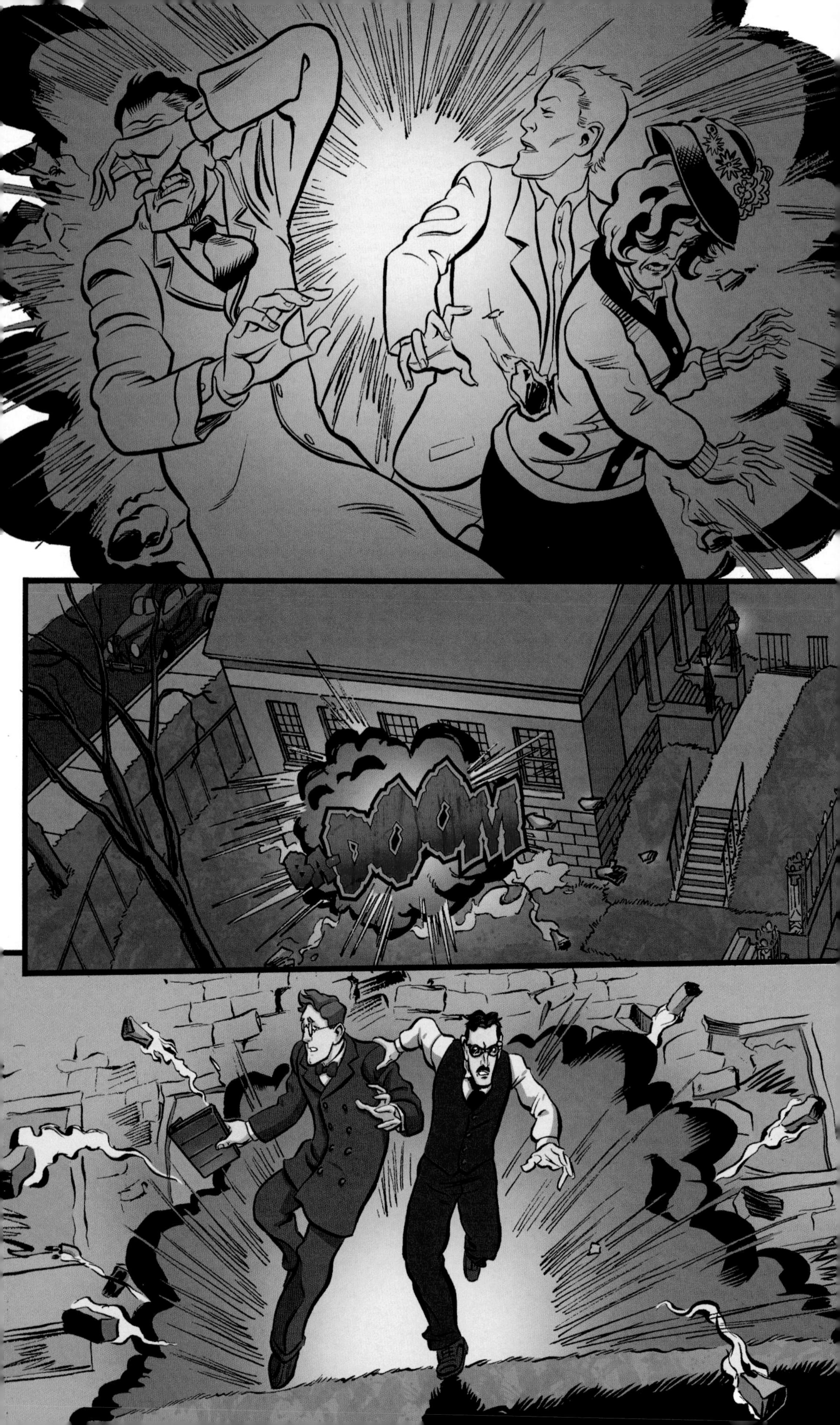
BA-DOOM

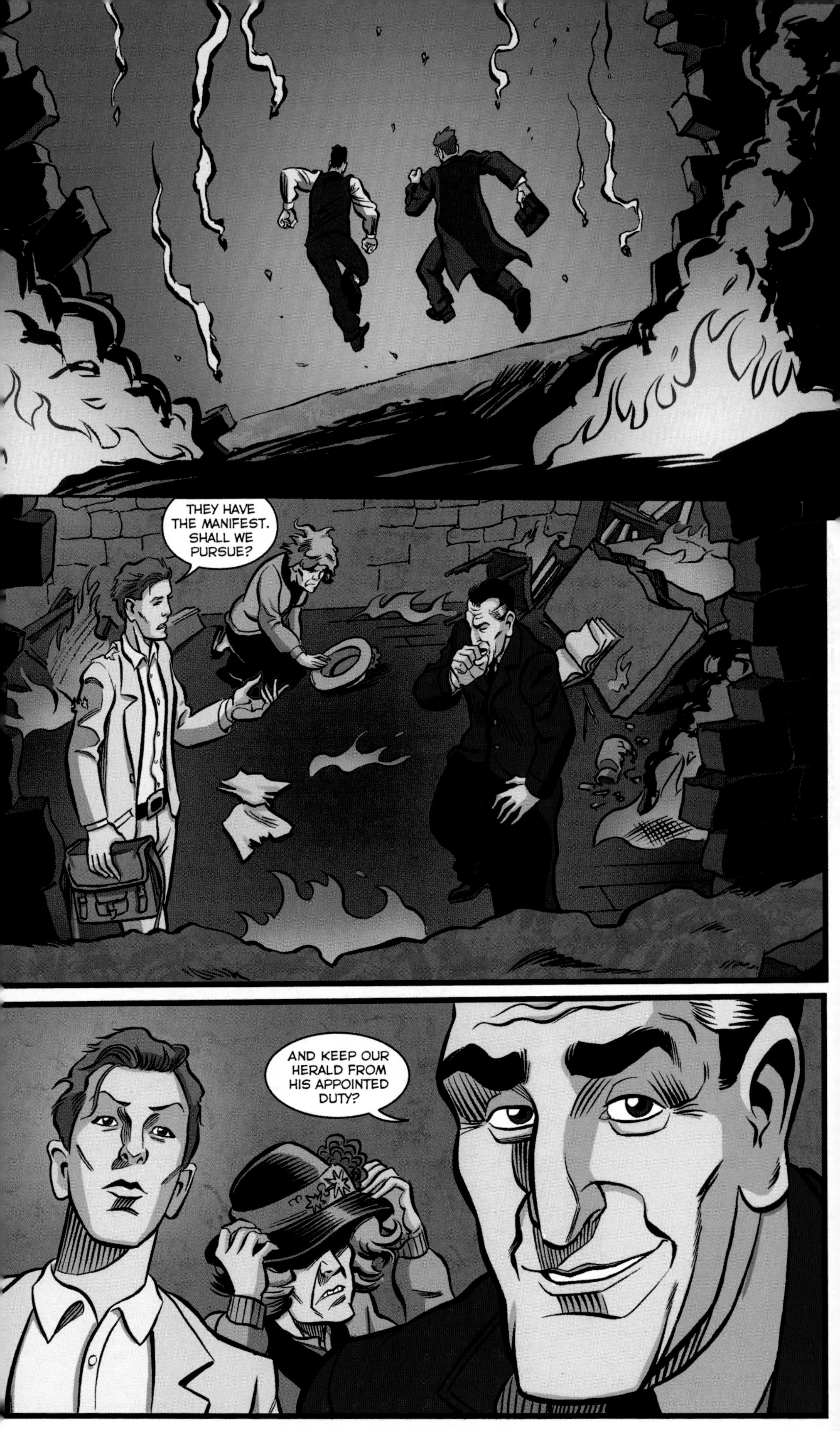
THEY HAVE THE MANIFEST. SHALL WE PURSUE?
AND KEEP OUR HERALD FROM HIS APPOINTED DUTY?

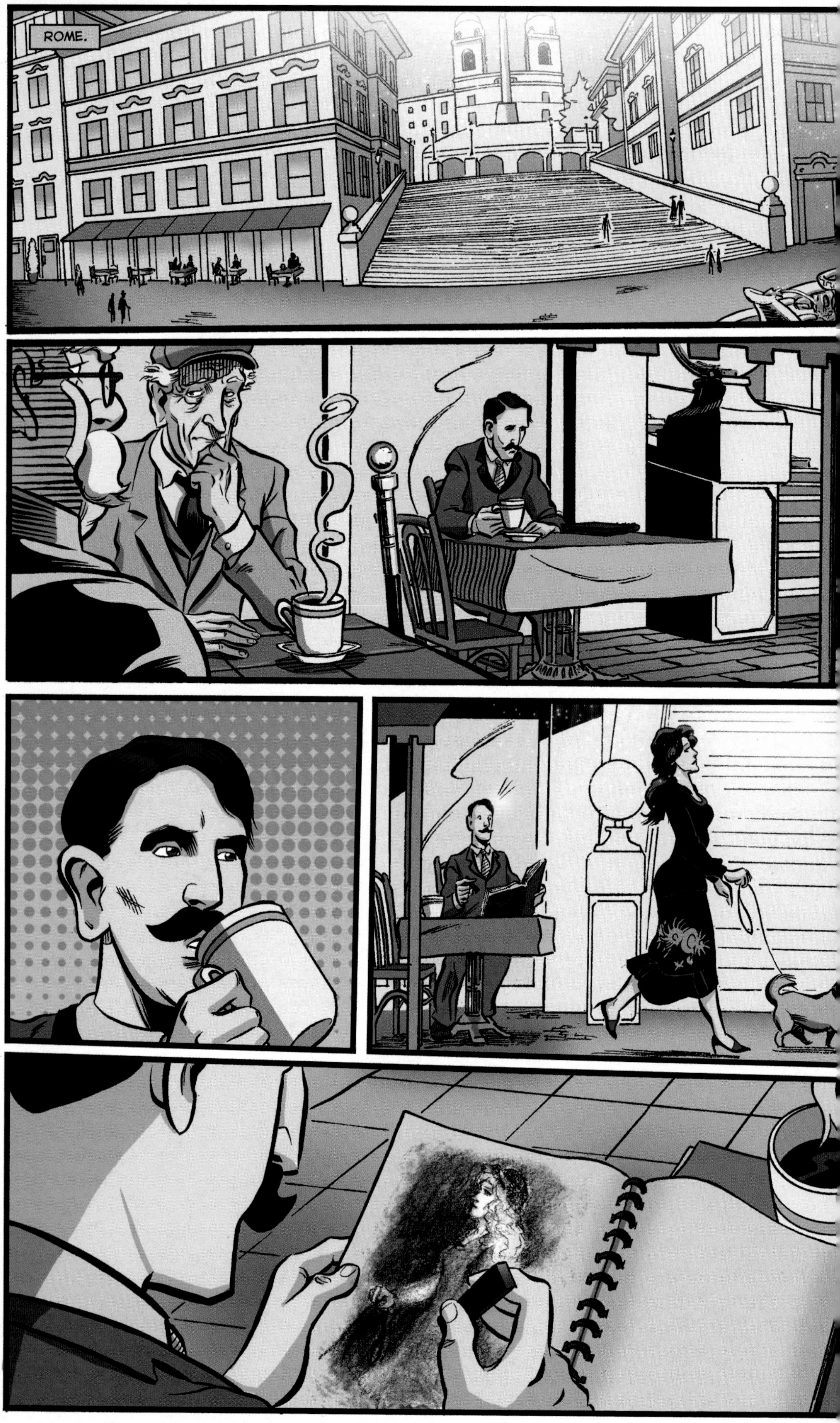
ROME.

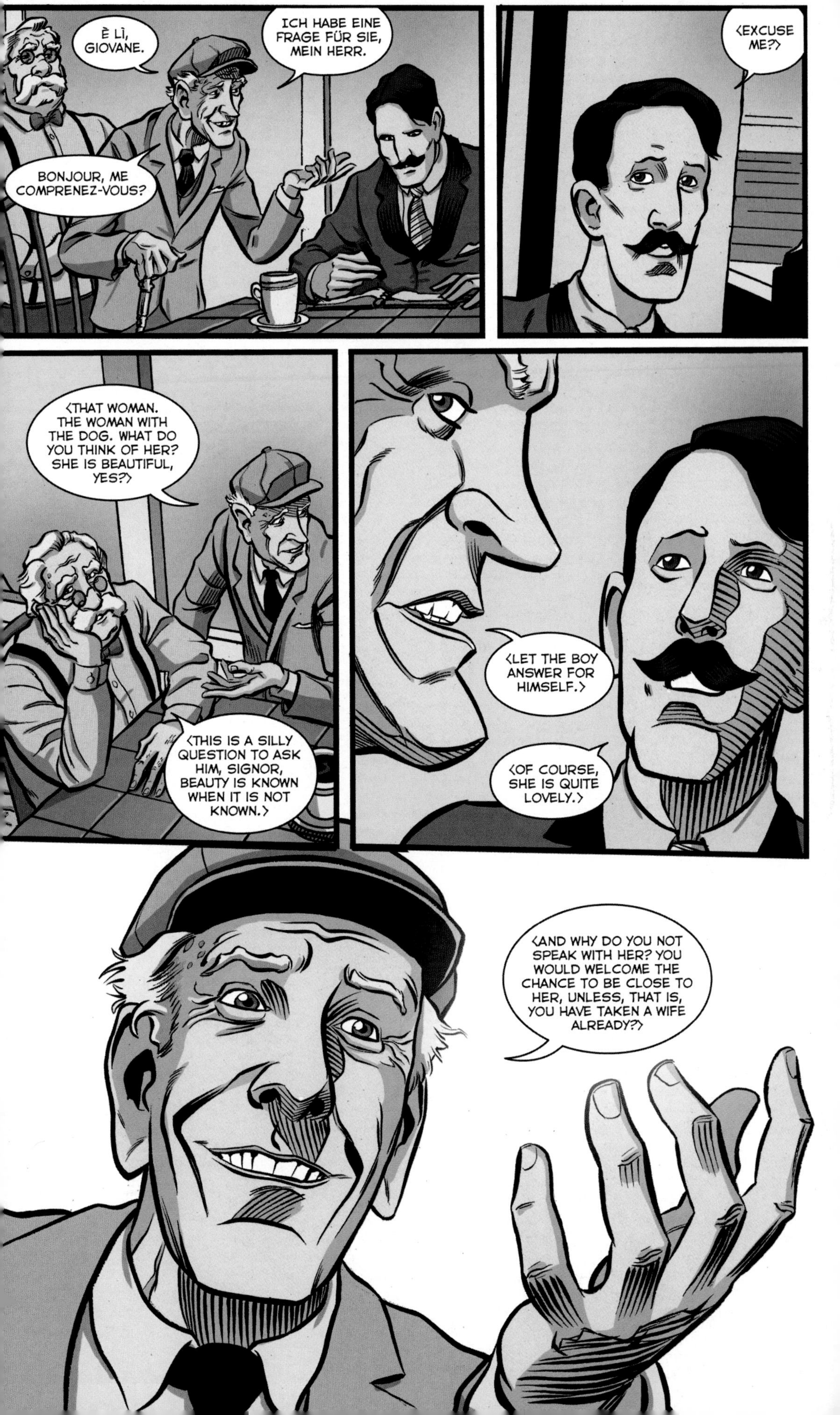
È LÌ, GIOVANE.
ICH HABE EINE FRAGE FÜR SIE, MEIN HERR.
BONJOUR, ME COMPRENEZ-VOUS?
<EXCUSE ME?>
<THAT WOMAN. THE WOMAN WITH THE DOG. WHAT DO YOU THINK OF HER? SHE IS BEAUTIFUL, YES?>
<THIS IS A SILLY QUESTION TO ASK HIM, SIGNOR, BEAUTY IS KNOWN WHEN IT IS NOT KNOWN.>
<LET THE BOY ANSWER FOR HIMSELF.>
<OF COURSE, SHE IS QUITE LOVELY.>
<AND WHY DO YOU NOT SPEAK WITH HER? YOU WOULD WELCOME THE CHANCE TO BE CLOSE TO HER, UNLESS, THAT IS, YOU HAVE TAKEN A WIFE ALREADY?>

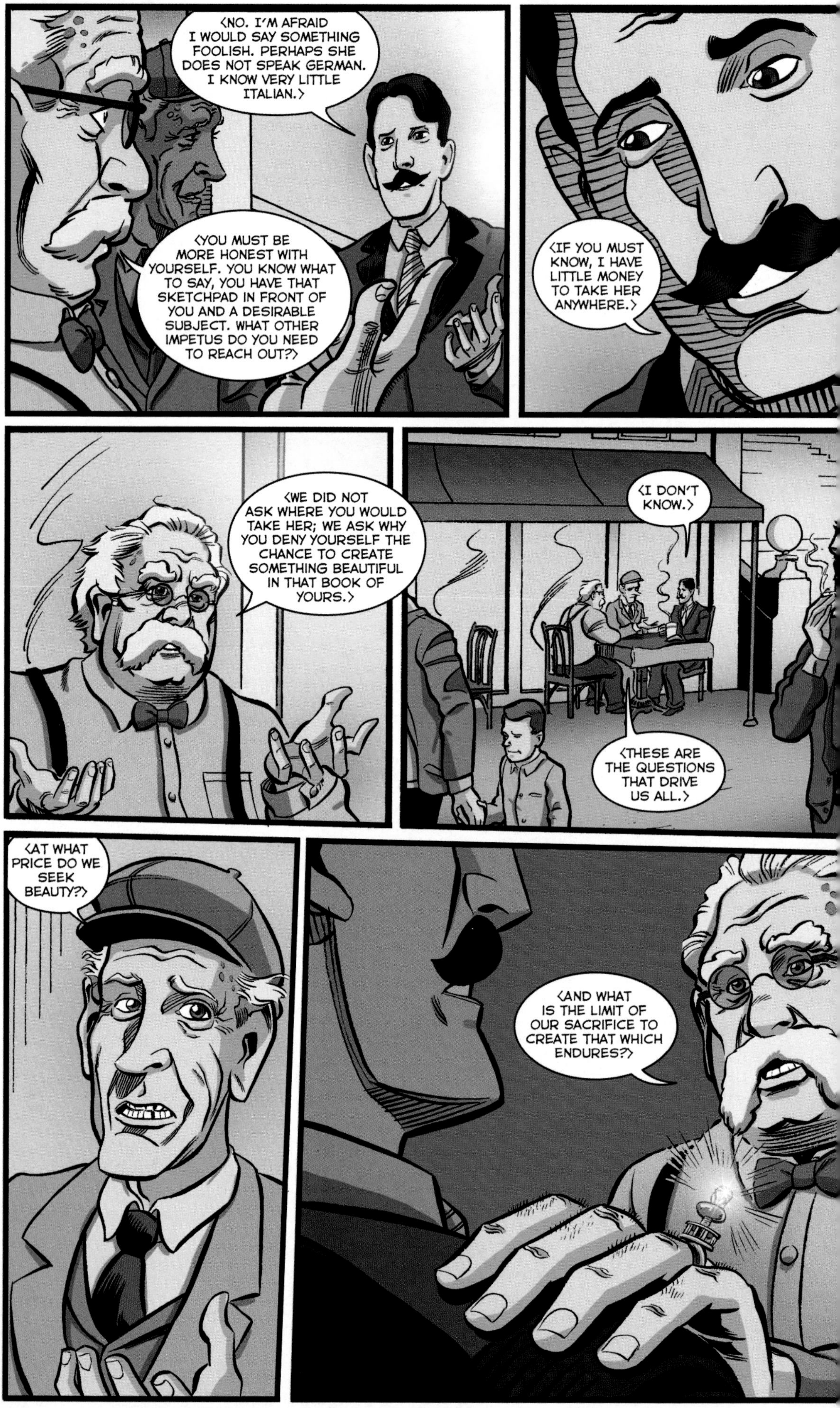
<NO. I'M AFRAID I WOULD SAY SOMETHING FOOLISH. PERHAPS SHE DOES NOT SPEAK GERMAN. I KNOW VERY LITTLE ITALIAN.>
<YOU MUST BE MORE HONEST WITH YOURSELF. YOU KNOW WHAT TO SAY, YOU HAVE THAT SKETCHPAD IN FRONT OF YOU AND A DESIRABLE SUBJECT. WHAT OTHER IMPETUS DO YOU NEED TO REACH OUT?>
<IF YOU MUST KNOW, I HAVE LITTLE MONEY TO TAKE HER ANYWHERE.>
<WE DID NOT ASK WHERE YOU WOULD TAKE HER; WE ASK WHY YOU DENY YOURSELF THE CHANCE TO CREATE SOMETHING BEAUTIFUL IN THAT BOOK OF YOURS.>
<I DON'T KNOW.>
<THESE ARE THE QUESTIONS THAT DRIVE US ALL.>
<AT WHAT PRICE DO WE SEEK BEAUTY?>
<AND WHAT IS THE LIMIT OF OUR SACRIFICE TO CREATE THAT WHICH ENDURES?>

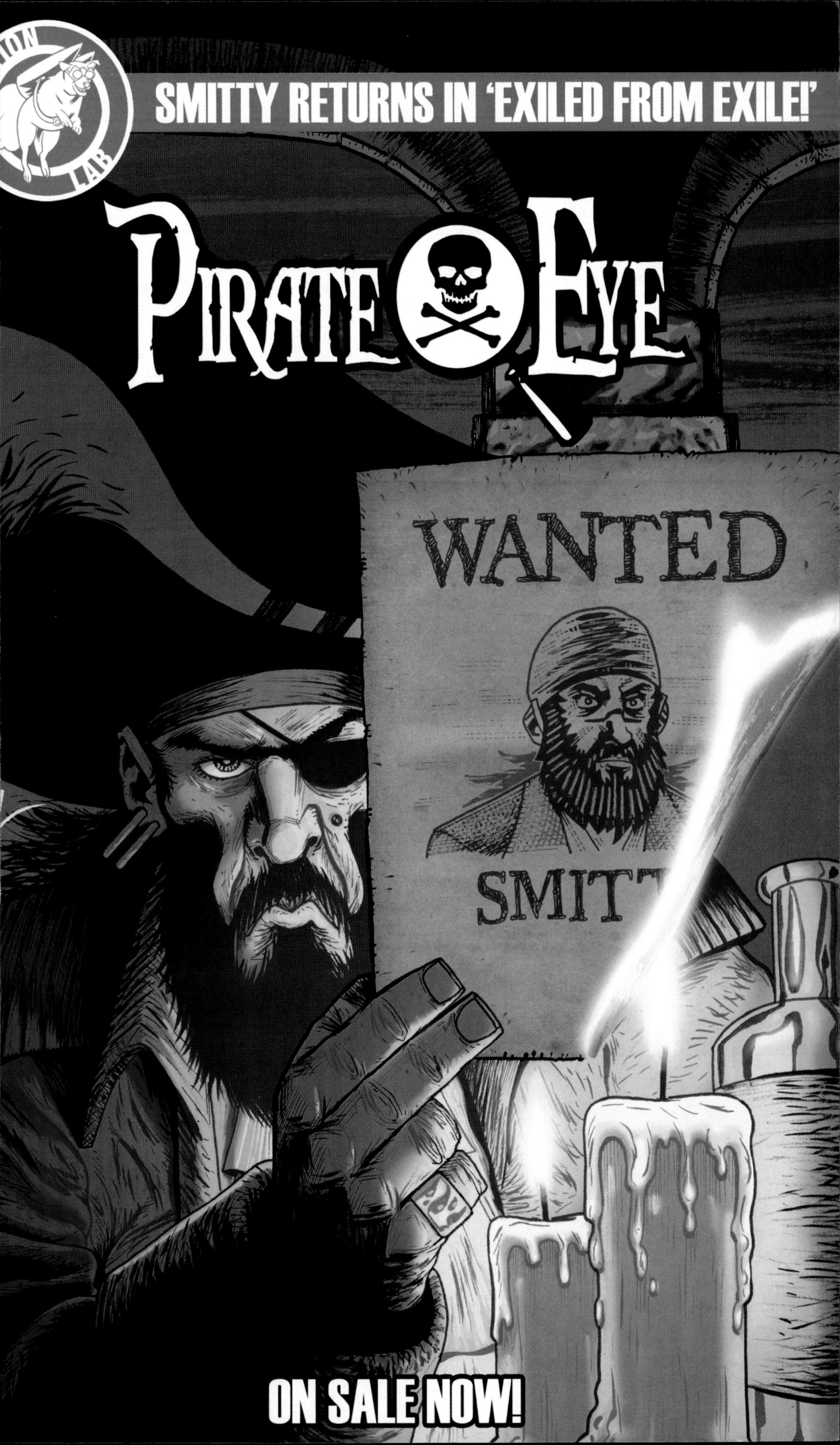
SMITTY RETURNS IN 'EXILED FROM EXILE!'
PIRATE EYE
WANTED
SMITT
ON SALE NOW!

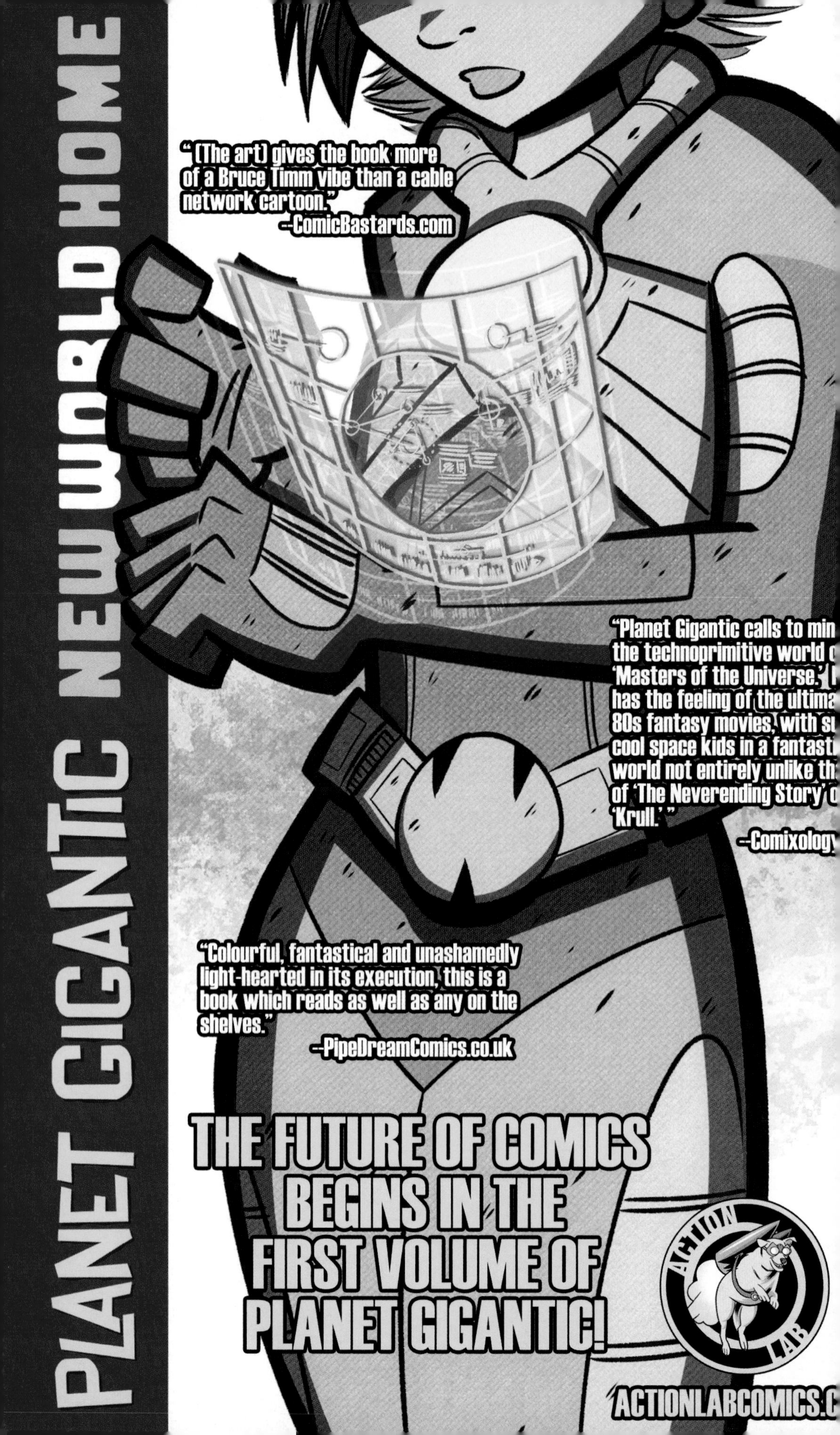

PLANET GIGANTIC NEW WORLD HOME
"(The art) gives the book more of a Bruce Timm vibe than a cable network cartoon."
--ComicBastards.com
"Planet Gigantic calls to min
the technoprimitive world o
'Masters of the Universe.' I
has the feeling of the ultima
80s fantasy movies, with su
cool space kids in a fantasti
world not entirely unlike th
of 'The Neverending Story' o
'Krull.'"
--Comixology
"Colourful, fantastical and unashamedly light-hearted in its execution, this is a book which reads as well as any on the shelves."
--PipeDreamComics.co.uk
THE FUTURE OF COMICS BEGINS IN THE FIRST VOLUME OF PLANET GIGANTIC!
ACTION LAB
ACTIONLABCOMICS.C

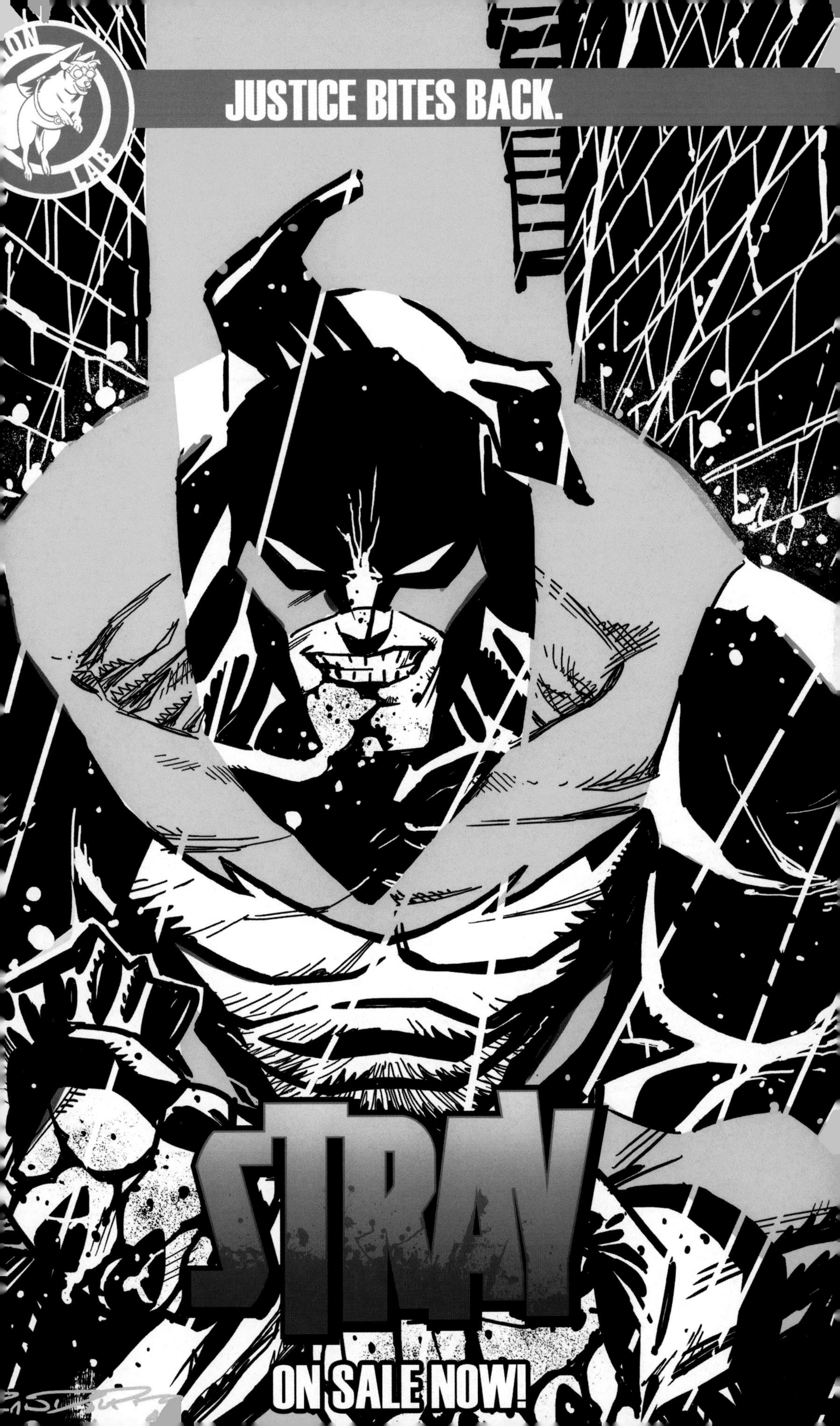
JUSTICE BITES BACK.
STRAY
ON SALE NOW!

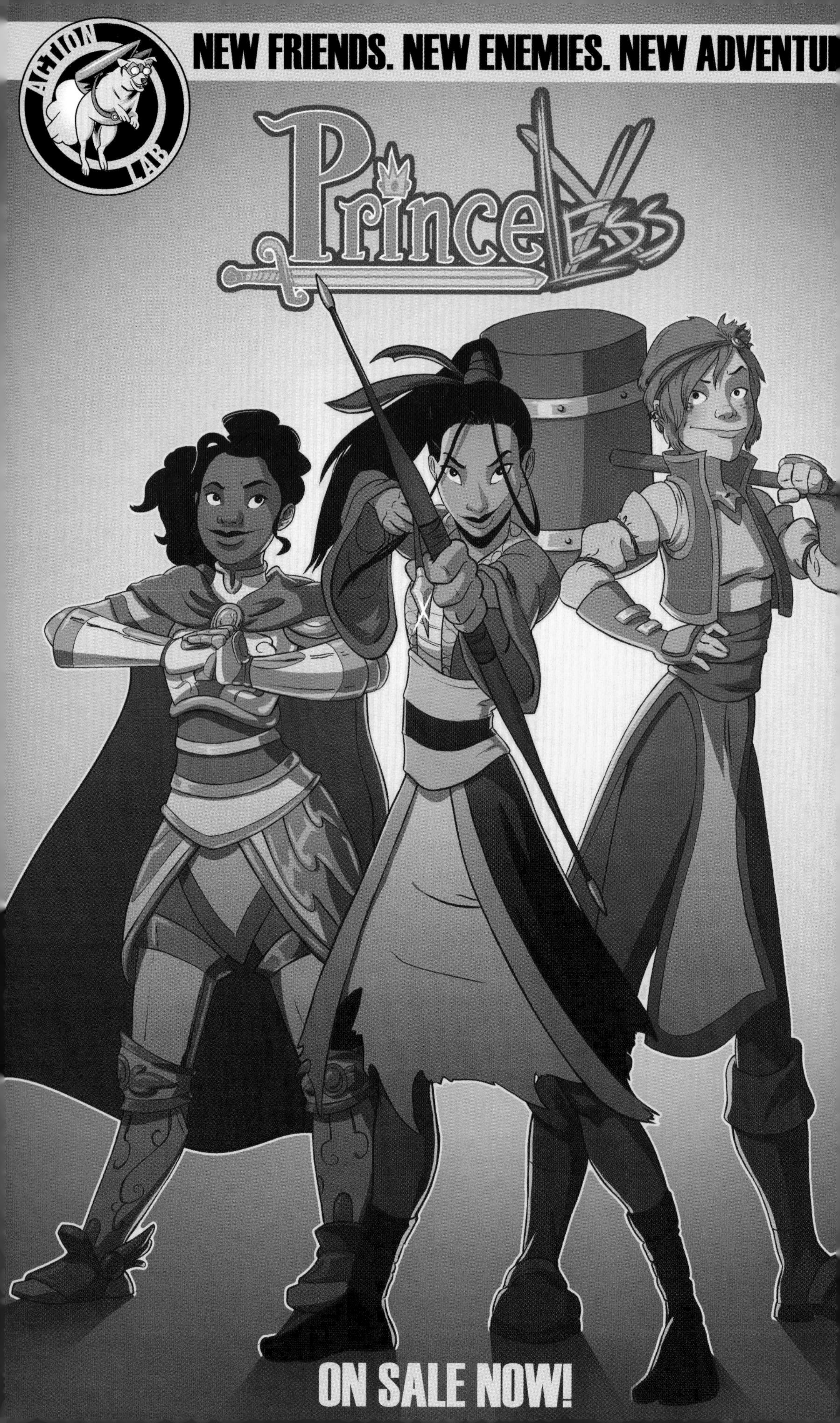
ACTION LAB
NEW FRIENDS. NEW ENEMIES. NEW ADVENTU
PrinceLESS
ON SALE NOW!

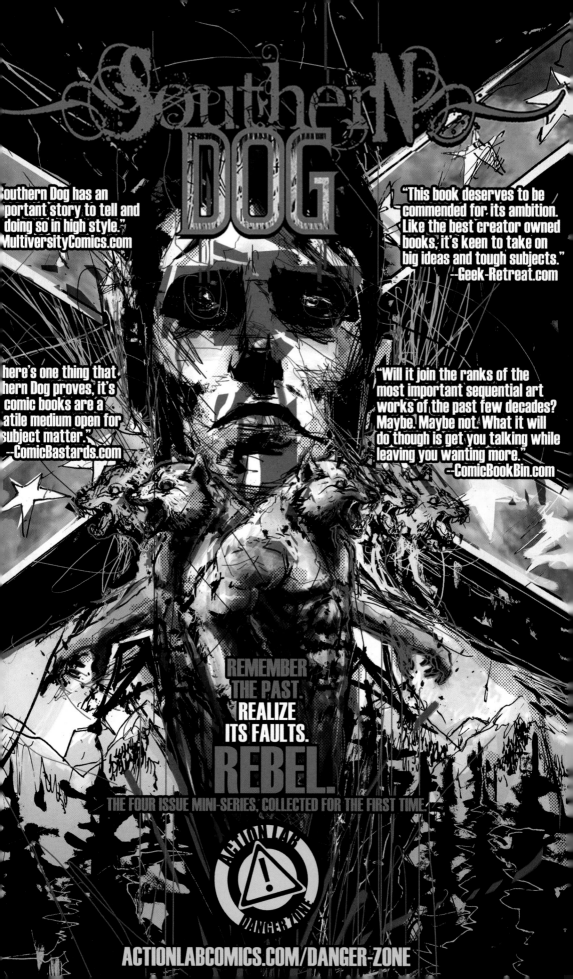

southern
DOG

"outhern Dog has an
portant story to tell and
doing so in high style."
MultiversityComics.com

"This book deserves to be
commended for its ambition.
Like the best creator owned
books, it's keen to take on
big ideas and tough subjects."
--Geek-Retreat.com

here's one thing that
hern Dog proves, it's
comic books are a
atile medium open for
subject matter."
--ComicBastards.com

"Will it join the ranks of the
most important sequential art
works of the past few decades?
Maybe. Maybe not. What it will
do though is get you talking while
leaving you wanting more."
--ComicBookBin.com

REMEMBER
THE PAST.
REALIZE
ITS FAULTS.
REBEL.

THE FOUR ISSUE MINI-SERIES, COLLECTED FOR THE FIRST TIME.

ACTION LAB
DANGER ZONE

ACTIONLABCOMICS.COM/DANGER-ZONE

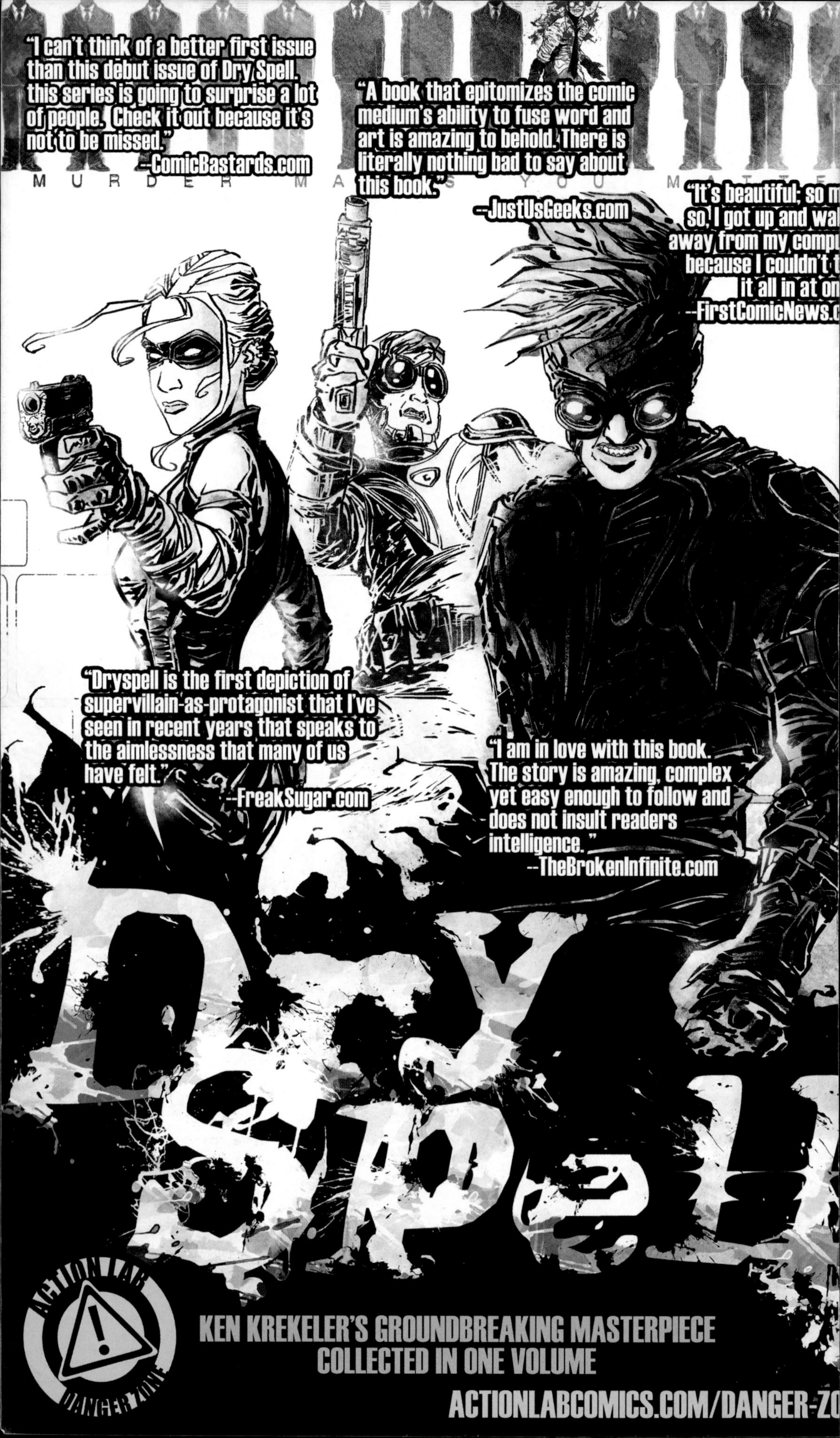
"I can't think of a better first issue than this debut issue of Dry Spell. this series is going to surprise a lot of people. Check it out because it's not to be missed."
--ComicBastards.com
"A book that epitomizes the comic medium's ability to fuse word and art is amazing to behold. There is literally nothing bad to say about this book."
--JustUsGeeks.com
"It's beautiful; so m
so, I got up and wal
away from my compu
because I couldn't t
it all in at on
--FirstComicNews.c
"Dryspell is the first depiction of supervillain-as-protagonist that I've seen in recent years that speaks to the aimlessness that many of us have felt."
--FreakSugar.com
"I am in love with this book. The story is amazing, complex yet easy enough to follow and does not insult readers intelligence."
--TheBrokenInfinite.com
ACTION LAB
DANGER ZONE
KEN KREKELER'S GROUNDBREAKING MASTERPIECE
COLLECTED IN ONE VOLUME
ACTIONLABCOMICS.COM/DANGER-ZO

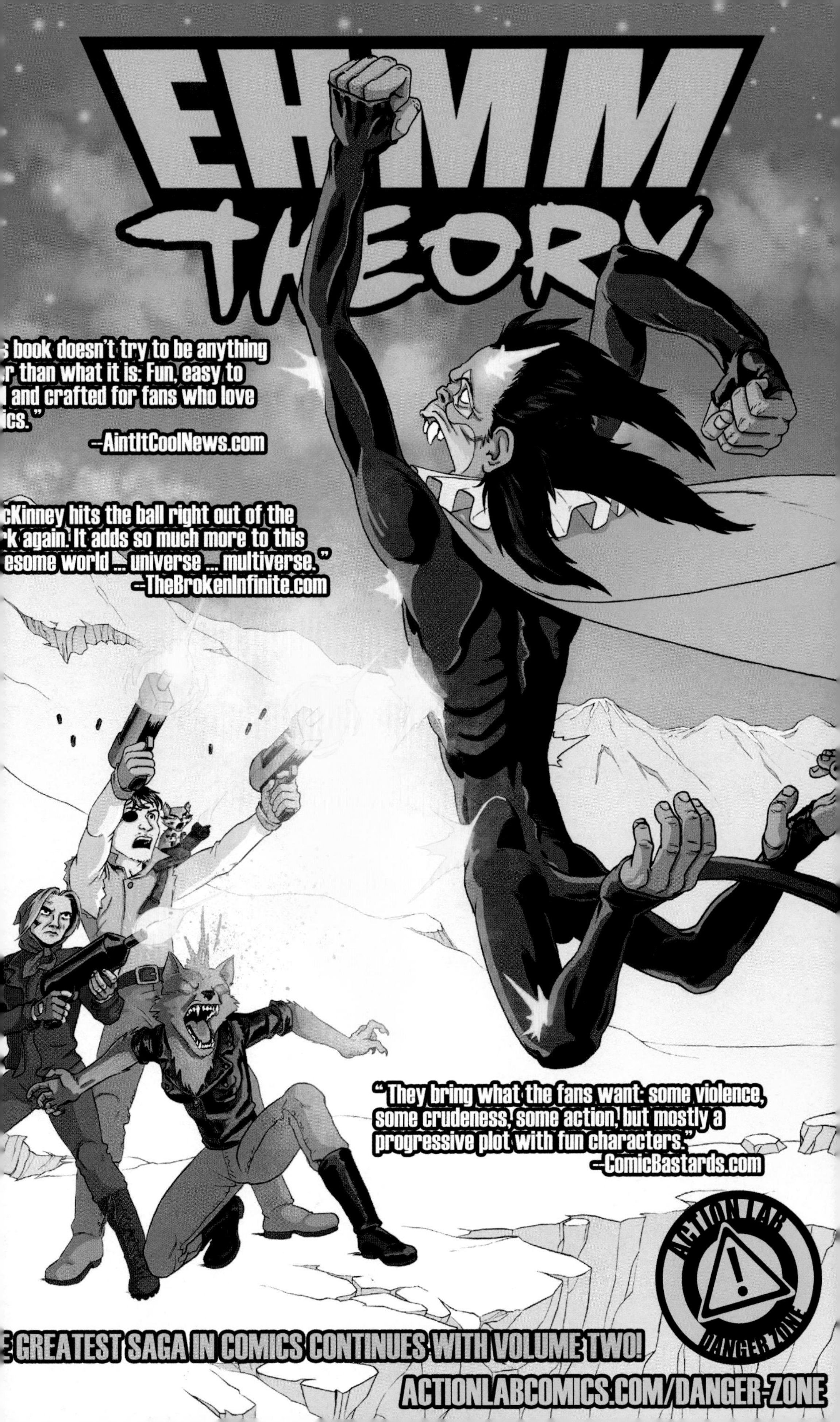
EHMM THEORY
s book doesn't try to be anything
r than what it is: Fun, easy to
and crafted for fans who love
ics."
--AintItCoolNews.com
cKinney hits the ball right out of the
'k again. It adds so much more to this
esome world ... universe ... multiverse."
--TheBrokenInfinite.com
"They bring what the fans want: some violence, some crudeness, some action, but mostly a progressive plot with fun characters."
--ComicBastards.com
ACTION LAB
DANGER ZONE
E GREATEST SAGA IN COMICS CONTINUES WITH VOLUME TWO!
ACTIONLABCOMICS.COM/DANGER-ZONE